The Life of Blessed Gabriel of Our Lady of Sorrows

*Rev. Hyacinth Hage, C.P. and
Rev. Nicholas Ward, C.P.*

Permissu Superiorum:
Stanislaus Grennan,
Provincialis, C.P.

Nihil Obstat:
Jacobus F. Loughlin, S.T.D.
Censor Librorum.

Imprimatur:
✠ *Patritius Joannes,*
Archiep. Philadelphien.

Imprimatur:
✠ *Edmundus Franciscus,*
Archiep. Philadelphien.

Original Name of Work:
The Life of Blessed Gabriel of Our Lady of Sorrows
Of the Congregation of the Passion
Begun by Rev. Hyacinth Hage, C.P.
Rewritten and enlarged by Rev. Nicholas Ward, C.P.
With an Introduction by Cardinal Gibbons
Copyright 1910, by H. L. Kilner & Co.

Retypeset and very lightly edited by Douglas Patterson.
Typesetting intentionally possesses no copyright.

Cover image taken from Wikipedia and cropped; licensed with CC BY-SA 4.0: (https://creativecommons.org/licenses/by-sa/4.0/)

Plan of Work

SECULAR LIFE
- Youth
- Childhood
- Vocation

RELIGIOUS LIFE
- Novitiate
- Scholasticate

WORK OF PERFECTION
- Cardinal Virtues
  - Temperance
  - Justice
  - Fortitude
  - Prudence
- Theological Virtues
  - Faith
  - Hope
  - Charity

MEANS OF PERFECTION
- Evangelical Counsels
- Mental Prayer
  - Devotion to Passion
  - Devotion to Mary
  - Communion of Saints

CONSUMATION IN DEATH

GLORIFICATION
- Introduction of Cause
- Voice from Heaven
- Judgment of Church
- Beatification

Protestation

The following pages are the result of a long and loving study of all the biographical material in French and Italian; but the volume is founded principally upon the sworn depositions contained in the Episcopal and Apostolical Processes.

It must be specially noted that every testimony quoted, and every instance of miracle or prodigy related, are faithful extracts from those official documents.

Mindful however of the decree of Urban VIII, I hereby disclaim any intention of anticipating the final judgment of the Church concerning this account of the life, virtues or miracles of the Bl. Servant of God, Gabriel of the Virgin of Dolors. This public and official judgment has already been commenced, by the promulgation of the decree of his solemn beatification in St. Peter's, Rome, on May 31, 1908, and it will be completed on the day of his future canonization, whenever God wills.[1]

Nicholas Ward, C.P.

St. Michael's Monastery,

West Hoboken, NJ

---

[1] Editor's Note: The Church solemnly canonized Saint Gabriel of Our Lady of Sorrows on May 13, 1920.

Contents

Introduction by Cardinal Gibbons 7
1 ***Birth and Parentage*** 12
2 ***Childhood*** 16
3 ***Youth and School Life*** 24
4 ***Religious Vocation*** 31
5 ***His Journey to the Novitiate*** 44
6 ***Life in the Novitiate*** 51
7 ***His Affections Spiritualized*** 64
8 ***His Clerical Studies*** 69
9 ***The Struggle for Perfection*** 74
10 ***Temperance and Mortification*** 81
11 ***Chastity*** 88
12 ***His Humility*** 94
13 ***His Meekness*** 102
14 ***His Cheerfulness*** 105
15 ***His Spirit of Religion*** 110

16 *His Regularity*	117
17 *His Spiritual Courage*	121
18 *His Prudence*	127
19 *His Spirit of Faith*	138
20 *His Lively Hope*	142
21 *His Ardent Charity*	145
22 *His Love of God*	150
23 *The Evangelical Counsels*	158
24 *His Spirit of Prayer*	165
25 *His Devotion to the Passion*	172
26 *His Devotion to Mary*	177
27 *Other Special Devotions*	190
28 *His Last Illness*	195
29 *His Holy Death*	204
30 *His Growing Fame*	212
31 *Our Latest Wonder-Worker*	219
32 *What Gabriel Has Done For Isola*	245
33 *His Solemn Beatification*	248

Introduction by Cardinal Gibbons

Mere natural virtue, however excellent and praiseworthy, can never raise man to the sublime perfection which is the end of his creation. Divine faith and grace joined with man's co-operation, alone justify the soul unto eternal salvation. "If thou wilt enter into life, keep the commandments" (Matthew 19:17); and the first and the greatest commandment is: "Thou shalt love the Lord thy God with thy whole heart." (Mark 12, Matthew 22) No other plan of salvation has God ever given, either in the old dispensation or in the new. To facilitate the road to this perfection, Christ gave His disciples the evangelical counsels of poverty, continency and obedience, and when accepted as irrevocable obligations, they place the disciple in a new state of life, which is therefore, the state of perfection. "If thou wilt be perfect," said Christ to the young man, "go sell what thou hast, and give to the poor, and thou shalt have treasure in heaven, and come, follow Me." (Matthew 19:21) It was from among those who had left all things to follow Him, that He chose His apostles. Here unto likewise, He invited Christians in every age, when he said: "Every one that hath left house or brethren or sisters, or father or mother, or wife or children or lands for My name's sake, shall receive a hundredfold, and shall possess life everlasting." (Matthew 19:29) In these passages of the gospel, Christian tradition has ever seen the institution of the state of perfection, which the Church of God has prudently adapted to the circumstances of place and time, embodying it in various rules and constitutions, just as she has acted with relation to the sacraments, surrounding them with appropriate rites and ceremonies.

Thus were the different forms of the religious life introduced: eremitic and monastic, clerical and lay; wherein a steadily increasing number of Christians, male and female, dedicated themselves to the exercises of the contemplative or active life. Apart from this variety of forms, one thing ever remained common to all, as the very essence of the state of perfection, namely an irrevocable profession of the three evangelical counsels, whereby the state of perfection became synonymous with the religious state, and those who professed it became *religious* properly so-called.

From the earliest times, too, the Church accepted this profession in God's name, regarded the whole religious life as a state of consecration, and those that belonged to it as sacred: insomuch that the same canon law that protected the Church's ministers from violence also safeguarded the religious, and rendered him that profaned the person of a religious or a cleric, equally guilty of sacrilege.

So complete is the sacrifice implied by the religious profession, that the early fathers have compared it to a holocaust, the victim of which dies to the world to live only for God. The world assumes that such self-annihilation is of no public utility: but "if the grain of wheat falling into the ground die, it bringeth forth much fruit," (John 12:24) and every unprejudiced observer may infer the rich harvest of beneficent works accruing to the general public from religious in the past, from what is now accomplished by the numerous religious institutions that dot the fair territory of these United States.

In the life of the youthful Passionist now presented for the first time to American readers, the excellence of the religious state is plainly set forth in a more than ordinary degree. A child of our own times, whose days barely cover twenty-four years of the middle of this expiring century, the sanctity of the Bl. Gabriel Possenti has been made illustrious by the wonders wrought at his grave since 1892. His early life presents this unique feature, that it contained no presage of his future holiness until he crossed the threshold of his cloister-home. The five short years in which the work of his spiritual perfection was accomplished, were spent in the obscurity of the retreat, devoted to the performance of common duties, as if God wished to emphasize once more in the eyes of the world, the sanctifying efficacy of the religious state.

Moved by these considerations, no sooner was the extraordinary virtue of this Servant of God brought to my notice, than I conceived for the youthful hero a love and admiration which were but the outcome of my profound esteem for the religious state. I recall with pleasure that in 1895, together with our illustrious brethren in the Sacred College, Cardinal Parocchi of Rome, and Cardinal Vaughan of London, I was one of the three bishops who first petitioned the Holy See for Gabriel's beatification. I then represented to the Sovereign Pontiff "what honor would thereby accrue to the Church, what salutary profit to Christian people, and especially what assistance to youth, so sorely straightened in these days by the spirit of wickedness." (Epistola Postulat, Aug. 4th, 1895) Similar petitions have since been forwarded to the Holy Father by twenty-nine cardinals, and as many archbishops and bishops; and now that the petition has been granted, we gladly introduce to the public this "Life of the Venerable Gabriel, of the Passionist Congregation."

Besides, this little volume is a new departure in hagiography, and one to be commended. A glance at the fundamental plan which underlies the work will reveal the object of the author. After the historical portion that leads up to Gabriel's correspondence to his religious vocation, we follow step by step, the development of his interior perfection. Helped by divine grace, and guided by a wise and prudent director, the young religious applies himself first to overcome the passions of rebellious nature, passing thence to the acquisition of the moral virtues that form the character of the man. Thus we come to sympathize with Gabriel as a brother, before we are consciously drawn to admire and imitate the saint. The heart being thus purified and strengthened, free scope is given to the operations of grace, which works by faith, hope and charity, unto the perfect union with God wherein consists our supreme perfection. Then only are we shown how marvelously this work was fostered by the means proper to the state of perfection, until we see its consummation in a holy death, and its wonderful sanction by the voice of heaven.

Whilst showing the excellence of the religious life, it is hoped that this little book will be an encouragement to those whose vocation is in the world, showing them that holiness is not to be sought for in wonderful deeds, but rather in the ordinary duties of life when sanctified by the love of God: in this alone, *essential perfection* consists.

To those who overestimate the value of moral virtue, it will show that this is only *consequent perfection*; that is, valuable only in proportion to the amount of grace and divine charity that animates it; bereft of which, the most heroic deeds are deserving only of human praise, and an earthly reward.

Let us add, in conclusion, that for those more privileged souls who live in the cloister, this little book will be a gentle reminder that the religious state, as such, is not ready-made sanctity put on with the religious habit, but only a means (*instrumental perfection*, as theologians call it) to be used unto an end—the acquisition of virtue.

J. Card. Gibbons

Baltimore, Feast of St. Aloysius, 1899.

J. X. P.[2]

The Life of Blessed Gabriel of the Sorrowful Mother, of the Congregation of the Passion.

1 Birth and Parentage

"Do you wish to enjoy in the loveliest season of the year the spectacle of one of the most beautiful regions of far-famed Italy? Then, traverse by slow stages the road which leads from Florence to Arezzo and Cortona, thence along the classic and enchanted shores of Lake Thrasymene to Perugia, and then down the eastern slopes of the mountains overlooking the Tiber to the mountain-side beyond, to whose steep acclivities clings Assisi." Here it was, that on the first day of March, 1838, was born of Sante Possenti and Agnes Frisciotti, a child who in these dark days was to enhance the ancient splendor of Umbria by adding one star more to the constellation which has made this province the land of sweetest saints. The late bishop of Assisi, Nicanor Priori, a truly holy man wrote: "Even as this city, in the most troublous times of the church, brought

---

[2] Editor's Note: These letters stand for "Jesu XPI Passio," the words on the Passionist Sign. Taken from Greek and Latin, it means "The Passion of Jesus Christ."

forth the Blessed Francis and other men of great holiness forechosen of God, that by their splendor and example they might enkindle the faith, purify the morals, and by the foolishness of the cross confound the wisdom of the world,—even so, in these latter and more evil times, did it give birth to another Francis,[3] surnamed Possenti (and afterward among the Fathers of the Passion, Gabriel of the Sorrowful Virgin,)—who having followed the example of the first, showed himself principally to the young, a despiser of the world, a follower of all good works, and an ardent lover of the Cross of Christ." His father, Sante Possenti, was a lawyer of exceptional talent, who during his long life of eighty-two years, deserved well of his native land. When barely twenty-two years old, Signor Possenti was appointed governor of Urbania in Romagna. He was continued in this office in various places, with successive promotion, by five Popes, until in 1842, Gregory XVI nominated him Grand Assessor of Spoleto, in which capacity he continued to serve his country up to the date of his retirement from public life in 1858.

His mother belonged to one of the most conspicuous families of Civitanova in the Marches; but the distinctions of fortune and birth were enhanced in her by a treasure far more precious and praiseworthy—the blessing of a lively faith, shining forth in works of charity and religion. The union of this distinguished couple was a happy one, and God blessed them with a numerous family, thirteen in all, four of whom received

---

[3] Editor's Note: St. Gabriel's birth name in his native tongue of Italian is 'Francesco.'

the crown of innocence in their tender years, all the rest walked in the footsteps of their holy parents, two being raised to the priesthood; while Francis, the eleventh of their children, was destined to be the brightest gem in the diadem of their parental love. Happy the parents of virtuous children! Blessed the children of true Christian parents!

Following the laudable custom of Catholic countries, Francis was baptized on the very day of his birth, and by a gracious dispensation of Providence, he was regenerated at the same font where eight hundred years before, the glorious patriarch of Assisi, St. Francis, had been born to grace. Our little Francis was entrusted to a nurse during the first year of his life, on account of the delicate health of his good mother, but on his father receiving the appointment of Governor of Montalto in 1839, the child was restored to his family. The official duties of the father, as well as the frequent changes of residence implied in his various appointments, left him but little time to share either the burdens or pleasures of home-life; but his devoted wife consecrated herself with all the greater solicitude to the Christian education of her children; and already at so tender an age, she began to arouse in Francesco's infant soul the first awakenings of the faith and grace of his holy baptism.

At last the day dawned when in consequence of Signor Possenti's appointment to Spoleto, the loving parents might hope to live henceforth undisturbed in a permanent home. But alas, hardly had a few months passed by when one of the children, Rose, only seven months old, took her flight to join her two angel brothers Paul and Louis, in heaven; then, a few weeks later, Adele, a lovely maiden of nine summers, passed away; and finally after a melancholy interval of a few weeks, the bereaved family in deep mourning and sorrow laid the mortal remains of their beloved mother to rest. Agnes Frisciotti-Possenti, young in years but rich in merits, died February 9, 1842. She sleeps in the church of the Oratorians at Spoleto waiting for the day when she will shine before the world as *the mother of a saint.*

2 Childhood

God's providence has its mysterious ways—— the cross must try and perfect his elect. The widowed father bowed his head in tearful resignation, then with the solicitude of a mother and the fortitude of a Christian, he looked duty in the face undaunted. Surrounded by a family of nine children, the duties of his important office hardly left him time to sit at table in their midst; so, at last he resolved to entrust the government of his household, as well as the care of the family, to a respectable and experienced lady named Pacifica. The imputation of harshness which we find recorded of her may well be excused on the score of necessity, if we consider the age and number of the boys and girls committed to her charge; while time and results proved that Signor Possenti had not been mistaken in his choice, and the affection and respect ever shown her in after-life by his family, well attest how worthy she was of the absolute confidence placed in her. None, however, cherished a more grateful remembrance of her than Francis, as his letters amply attest.

At the very outset, we might as well inform our readers, that the child, whose life-story we have undertaken, did not in his early years manifest any of those extraordinary signs of precocious holiness so often found in the lives of the saints. In fact, Francis was, if anything, more lively than any of his brothers and sisters, and as he grew up, his gay and sympathetic nature brought more than its expected share to the noise and bustle of the Possenti mansion. Then, too, our hero was not without his faults. He began to show unmistakable signs of anger, giddiness, and disobedience. The impetuosity of his nature would often break out in fits of passion, which it was no easy matter for him to control. His earliest biographer states that when corrected by his father, Francesco would give way to his angry feelings, his face would become inflamed with the violence of his unruly temper, and he would leave the company abruptly. But the flame would subside almost as quickly as it had been enkindled; his better nature would assert itself, and then it was beautiful to see him after the absence of a few moments, return to his father, weeping and confused, begging pardon for his hastiness. But his father would pretend not to care for this change of feeling, and would dismiss him, saying: "Francesco, what I want, is that you learn to behave yourself." Then would the boy throw himself upon his father's neck, embrace and kiss him, until the parent, conquered and moved, would assure his son that he loved his dear little Francesco still. Blessed the son who learns betimes to revere and love his father! Filial affection will mould his character into manliness more effectually than the rod: the human reason unfolds only in the light of reason, the human heart is conquered only by the conviction of love.

Signor Possenti had not been slow to realize that his paternal admonitions, even when emphasized in his absence by a watchful and devoted governess, would hardly prove a sufficient aid and safeguard for his growing sons; so a tutor was selected for them, a young cleric of piety and ability, who should be to them an experienced friend and constant companion, guiding them in their studies and associating with them in all their recreations. Such a measure may appear strange to our American ideas of self-education, but it was a custom among families of rank and consideration in other days and other lands; and it will hardly be denied that habitual intercourse with a more trained and mature companion is likely to form a more manly character in the young, than if they grew up with those of their own age, and tastes, and dispositions. However, it is not our object to become the advocate of any system, depending as it must needs do, so largely upon national traits and local circumstances; suffice it to say that a worthy and congenial companion was provided for the young sons of Signor Possenti in the person of Philip Fabi. When he was installed in his new office he was ten years older than Francis, and survived him by many years. By reason therefore of his close intimacy, he became a valuable witness to his pupil's conduct as a secular, when the juridical processes were set on foot.

Fabi's task was by no means easy. About this time, we are told, that Francesco's character was very changeable; all inclined to piety one day, and on the morrow equally given up to worldliness: now all studiousness and fervor, then all tepidity and languor. Yet, in the midst of this fickleness, his piety would burst into sudden flame, revealing the fire of virtue that lay smoldering in his heart.

Let it not be supposed, however, that it was Signor Possenti's intention to give a private tuition to his sons: he was fully aware of the blessing of public education, and as the first magistrate of the city, he was too public-spirited to seek any for his boys but the common schools; he feared for them, not their contact with the poor, but the contamination of the wicked; and the advantages of select schools were far outweighed in his mind by the democratic idea of spirited emulation with talent and merit, in whatever class of society they might be found. His one ambition was to make his sons true men, useful citizens and practical Christians.

And so it came to pass that little Francis, to his supreme delight, found himself accompanying his older brothers on his way to school. At that time elementary education in Spoleto was superintended by the Brothers of the Christian Schools, and it was under the influence of their teaching and example that the seeds of virtue implanted in his soul by his Christian parents, developed into flowers and fruits, despite the weeds that threatened to stifle them.[4] "It was while under the care of the Christian Brothers," says his sister Teresa, "that Francis received the first rudiments of learning, as well as his first systematic instruction in religion. From his earliest school days," she continues, "he showed a special devotion to the Blessed Virgin, never missing the rosary that we recited at

---

[4] The idea of *public schools* is not an invention of our times or of our country: it is as old as the parish and cathedral communities in the Catholic Church. Its modern and popular form is derived from two of her illustrious sons: Peter Fourrier doing for the education of girls, what John Baptist de La Salle did for the boys. The society instituted by the latter to further Christian education (though but one of the many now flourishing in the Church of God) numbers at present about 18,000 religious, all pledged to the principle of gratuitous education.

home every evening. He often visited the sacred image or *Icon* of our Lady in the cathedral; and if perchance the doors were closed, he would devoutly venerate the statue placed over the entrance, *la santissima Vergine del Portico,* as it was called."

"My brother's moral conduct was ever unblemished," writes his Dominican brother, Louis, (who had lived with Francis until the latter had reached his twelfth year) "yet I remember that when he was very young he was not very strict in the custody of his eyes; it seems that little Francesco was a trifle too wide-awake; he thought it his prerogative to gratify his natural curiosity in seeing and knowing all things.

"Then, too, healthy boys are partial to fruits and sweets of all kinds, and our Francis was by no means an exception to the rule; but his generous nature would not enjoy what he could not share with others; and his sense of honesty was too deep-rooted to allow of his ever appropriating anything whatsoever that was not his own. The little fellow was, besides, full of courage. He could not bear to see anyone suffering unjustly, and full often he championed the cause of those older than himself, if they happened to be reprimanded or punished without reason. But on the other hand, his sense of justice would not allow to pass unnoticed any fault whether in the domestics, his brothers and sisters, or his companions; he was outspoken, perhaps even forward, but it was not hard to see that all this came from the uprightness of an honest heart.

"On the whole, Francis was both the terror and the favorite of the home, whilst his playful disposition made him a welcome companion to all his schoolmates. Usually rather careless about his personal appearance, he was not exempt from a tinge of vanity; still his heart was too magnanimous to receive any lasting impression from any kind of vulgar worldly show: with the same facility with which his eye would take to such things, he would put them aside, and sometimes disregard them with contempt, saying: 'O, after all, what do I care!'"

This nobility of character was not entirely due to the watchfulness of Pacifica, or to the influence of the good Brothers at school; most of it must be credited to Signor Possenti himself, in so many respects a model Christian father. This good man yielded to no one his place as the effective leader and teacher of his children, and he walked before them both by precept and example.

Signor Possenti was a man of piety and faith, and with the exercise of his religion he allowed nothing to interfere. Rising early in the morning, he began the day by devoting an entire hour to his morning devotions. He would afterward repair to the church to hear Holy Mass, taking with him most of his children. Then, relying on the assistance of God, and strengthened by the testimony of a good conscience, he would turn his attention to his judicial duties. This good Christian had likewise a remarkable love for the poor: both officially and privately he exerted himself to relieve their necessities, and he benefited by every occasion, not only to perform an act of charity, but to instill into the hearts of his children a practical sympathy for the suffering members of Christ. To the father's great delight, Francis learned the lessons of charity at the cost of personal self-denial. From his earliest years the boy showed great compassion for the poor, often giving away half of his lunch during the recess at school. Returning home, if he happened to meet some unfortunate creature whose misery moved him to pity, he would go at once to Pacifica, and ask for bread; but it sometimes happened that the good woman's generosity was not all commensurate with the demands that Francis saw fit to levy upon it; then would our young hero remonstrate with her, saying: "Why!...father wants us to be charitable; we ought not to despise the poor, for we don't know what we may one day be ourselves." In the evening, after the labors of the well-filled day, Signor Possenti was accustomed to gather his sons and daughters in his room, and after the recitation of the rosary in common, hold with them such converse as was appropriate to their age and their needs. In the intimacy of such conversations he would open his heart to them, inculcating those Christian principles, wise counsels, and useful maxims, that were to guide them on the path of life; he would speak to them of their duties toward God, of the respect and gratitude we owe to His Church, of the obedience commanded by parental authority; above all, he would inveigh with all the warmth of his affection against the dangers of bad company, and impress upon his children's minds the vanity of the world, and everything in it. Then having received the blessing of such a noble Christian father, they would retire to rest. Truly did the parental blessing rest upon his family; truly by such a blameless life did Sante Possenti deserve the love of his children, and the glorious title of *being the father of a saint*!

3 Youth and School Life

In 1823 Cardinal della Genga, a native of Spoleto, ascended the papal throne under the name of Leo XII, and one of the first things that claimed his attention and solicitude was to provide for the youth of his native city the very best of educators. Instruction is not education: the latter term implies the formation of the heart as well as the cultivation of the mind; and it must be remembered in the words of a solid thinker of our own day that the teacher's personality, far more than his learning, determines his value as an educator.[5] Thus the two great teaching orders of the Church came to Spoleto, the sons of La Salle and of Loyola, the Christian Brothers and the Jesuits. Under the patronage of Archbishop Mastai-Ferretti (afterward Pius IX) the Fathers of the Society flourished, so that, when in 1842 the Possenti family was established at Spoleto, their college was already illustrious by the fame of its professors and the number of its students.

Signor Possenti, who was highly cultured himself, rejoiced at this opportunity of affording his sons a liberal education, and in 1849 it came to pass that having finished his elementary course of instruction with the good Brothers, our Francis followed his elder brothers to the Jesuit College, until he graduated in philosophy at the age of eighteen. Under such accomplished masters, Francis made rapid progress in secular as well as sacred knowledge. His success in his studies may

---

[5] Life and Education. Chap. vi. (Bp. Spalding of Peoria, 1897)

be gauged by his acknowledged talent, and from the honorable place accorded him in public examinations. His name is often mentioned in the programs which it was usual to print at the "Distribution of Premiums." His brother Henry says that the prize in philosophy was awarded to him, and his sister Teresa is still in possession of a "medal of honor" won by Francis at the end of the scholastic course, when such distinctions were far from being common.

Our young hero had a bright and open mind together with a tenacious memory. He was certainly one of the aptest scholars, writes his professor of mental philosophy; and one of his companions, his senior in the Passionist novitiate, attests that he must have gone through his studies with great success, judging from the knowledge with which he was well furnished.

All this, however, was enhanced in Francis by external qualities that made his talents more valuable still. His directors used to select him as public reader both for the sodality and in the college church, when the catechism took place there on festivals. No one could surpass him in this exercise, both for readiness and inborn gracefulness. Nature had endowed him with a clear and sonorous voice, and while reading he was so penetrated with the author's meaning that he seemed less to repeat the sentiments of others than to express his own. Hence many foresaw in him the valiant missionary, recognizing in the graceful reader, the gifts of the distinguished preacher. He succeeded equally well in the academic dissertations and the classic authors, all which he would read with such feeling and naturalness that it almost seemed original declamation. Such is the testimony of Canon Bonaccia his college companion. As years went on, it became evident to all, that Francis Possenti was one of those who gave well-grounded hopes of brilliant success in his future career, whatever that professional career might be.

While commanding admiration, his natural distinction offended nobody, because his frank, noble and generous disposition drew all to him, and surrounded him with the sweet halo of affection and esteem. And no wonder, for, ever smiling, kind and obliging to all, respectful to his superiors, he became the favorite of the Spoletan College, as he was the sunshine of his own home. Yet these bright prospects were not unaccompanied with danger. How many a noble soul is deceived by the vanities of the world, and blinded by its concupiscence! Hence the warning of the beloved disciple: (John 2:14-15) "Young men, love not the world." The personal qualities of Signor Possenti, no less than the social standing consequent on his high office, brought him in contact with the most refined and educated classes of the city, and threw open to him and his children the drawing-rooms of the most aristocratic and wealthy. It was customary with the nobility of Spoleto to hold soirées, in which the earlier hours of the night would be given to the familiar discussion of some artistic or scientific topic, after which the junior portion of the assembly would make merry in plays, music or dancing. Though rather young, Francis would occasionally be allowed to accompany his brothers and sisters, and as was to be expected, his winning ways soon made him so desirable a guest, that they were loath to miss him. These gatherings had such a fascination for him, that he would beg his father to bring him to them, and Signor Possenti fully appreciating the welcome accorded to his son would yield to his importunity, until so marked was Francis' partiality to these entertainments that he came to be called among his college associates, *il damerino*, or, the society young man. Success in these soirées, and the private theatricals, which often formed their most prominent feature, increased in the heart of Francis a love for the stage. The brilliancy of the illuminated theatre, the splendid assembly, the realistic scenery and dramatic action, the symphony of the orchestra and the singing of the artists rendering the grand opera of the Italian masters,—all these had for him a fascination of which he was less conscious than those who observed him closely. Whatever may be said theoretically of the stage as a factor in popular education, are not its advantages outweighed by its dangers, especially to the young?

To these dangers, the boy added another, and one which proves most hurtful to a very large number; he took to the reading of novels and romances. Not that he ever took into his hands the vile literature that awakens and inflames the impure passions; indeed, the press and the stage were under strict surveillance in the pontifical domain; and we must add that such was Francesco's wisdom and prudence, that he would frequent no place, nor read any book without the knowledge of his father. However, the effects of the worldly spirit which was insinuating itself into his son, can hardly have escaped the vigilant eye of Signor Possenti; still less those of his zealous teachers, whose prudence could not so easily be blinded by affection; in fact, it became evident to his companions. Parenzi writes: "Francis had an ardent temperament much inclined to pastimes. The last two years he spent at Spoleto, he gave himself up to a life of amusement; he was fond of the theatre, the drawing-room and the dance, showing in his dress and manner a marked degree of downright vanity." "He was naturally disposed to noble deeds," writes Bonaccia, his enthusiastic companion, "but the beauty of his soul was clouded by levity and vanity. And why seek to conceal it? Francesco showed himself extravagant in his dress, which had to be in the latest fashion, his hair was carefully parted and perfumed, the least stain on his clothes would make him indignant; he was immoderately fond of company and taken up with frivolities; this was the predominant passion of his youth." Yet, this worldliness did not proceed from a soft, effeminate nature, for Francis was ever a boy among boys, always at home in a crowd of jovial companions; the vanity and extravagance of which we have spoken above, became noticeable only during the last period of his college life; and even then, only on those occasions (frequent though they were) when he appeared "in society." At other times, like other boys, he was rather negligent in his dress, and ready to take a leading part in every manly game and recreation. The Spoletan lads enjoyed walks over the hills that encircle the city, and when the season permitted, they would shoulder their guns, and attired in corduroy (somewhat after our football fashion) they would spend the day in the woods.

If athletic sports, like everything human, are accompanied with some dangers, their inconveniences are more than counterbalanced by the advantages they procure, and not the least of these is that they are a wholesome salt against moral corruption, by spending in healthy exercise the animal spirits of ardent youth, and training the boy into self-control and self-possession. How many owe to a great extent the chastity of their body and the purity of their soul to this discipline of the flesh!

"Albeit that Francis was fond of appearing in society," writes his brother Henry who lived eighteen years with him, "he never failed in that modesty and reserve, which he had learned from our good parents." Boys are fair judges of one another: the freedom with which they treat each other, gives them a clearer insight into one another's souls, than could be had by either parents or teachers. Yet, neither Francesco's brothers nor the companions of his school-days, ever witnessed anything in his conduct that even savored of indelicacy. But our young hero strove to merit the protection of heaven, in the midst of his dangers. He was a strict observer of all his practices of piety; never did he neglect his daily devotions; every morning he assisted at the Holy Sacrifice of the Mass; he did not fail to visit the Blessed Sacrament frequently; showed a particular devotion to the Sacred Passion of our Redeemer, and recited the rosary of our Lady every night. Join to this, his frequent reception of the Holy Sacraments and the evident fervor of his dispositions, testified to by his brother Henry and some of his companions.

Still, this conduct, however exemplary, would not have saved him from eventual ruin; for during the last years of his secular life the youth was evidently playing with danger, trifling with grace; and the abnormal mixture of worldliness with devotion could not go on indefinitely. "Certainly," remarks his first biographer, "if such a mode of life were longer to continue, the world would ultimately have prevailed, and great would have been its conquest."

4 Religious Vocation

It is but natural for a youth with life and prospects before him to cast his glance upon the world and make his plans; it is but the noble ambition of a man on the verge of the social battlefield to ask himself where is his post of duty; it is but meet for a Christian boy anxiously to pray and seek for counsel that he may know God's will, and fulfill his mission.

And yet of that future now so near at hand, Francis did not even seem to think; for his career he manifested no concern: but in truth this was the only thing, over which his candid nature drew the veil of secrecy, even with his most trusted friends. Had they but known!...Our Francis *was not* indifferent to his future prospects: he felt that the Lord Himself was asking for the complete sacrifice of his heart, that a career more glorious than worldly heroes dream of, was marked out for him. "How many times," writes Bonaccia, "do I remember seeing him during his thanksgiving after communion, his head bowed in deepest reverence, his hands clasped, his eyes moist with silent tears, as if he were pondering over some great thought, and maturing with God some great design."

The truth is that a struggle of some years' standing was going on in his heart, and in proportion to his seeming unfaithfulness to grace his vocation all the more clearly revealed itself: he who watched over Francesco's soul as its Master constantly reminded him of his duty, while he protected him from serious danger.

The first warning came under the form of a grievous sickness which brought him to death's door. In his distress, the child felt inspired to have recourse to God through Our Lady's intercession, promising that if she obtained his cure, he would spend the rest of his life in a religious order. The promise was seemingly accepted, for he rapidly recovered, and from that hour he enjoyed greater health and strength than ever before. But his cure led to nothing definite: he allowed the grace that he received to become barren. After the lapse of some years, Francis was roused from his apathy when the Lord afflicted him a second time. He was suffering from a severe inflammation of the throat: acute laryngitis. One night the inflammation became so great that respiration was failing, and feeling that he was smothering, without the ability to help himself or even cry for the assistance of others, he thought he was about to die. Suddenly he remembered a picture of the Jesuit martyr Blessed[6] Andrew Bobola, which he received from one of his masters. He at once wrapped the picture round his neck, begging Almighty God, through the merits of his servant, to rescue him from his peril, and solemnly renewing his promise to become a religious. Presently he fell into a gentle slumber, and awoke in the morning cured. The inflammation not only subsided, but had almost completely disappeared; his breathing was easy, and on the picture of the saint there was a stain of matter, as it were a token of the favor bestowed. This time his mind was made up: he presented himself to the Father

---

[6] Editor's Note: Now Saint

Provincial of the Jesuits, asking to be received into the Society, and his request was granted. But, alas! from day to day he deferred the fulfillment of his promise, until truth to say, Francis was once more under the spell of the secular world with all its works and pomps. He did not indeed, positively contradict God's inspirations; not for a moment did he doubt his vocation, but he was ever putting off to a future day the execution of his design. He was like one who, waking from sleep and remembering the call of duty, instead of rising instantly, gives way to his sloth, is overcome by drowsiness and falls asleep again. Despite all appearances to the contrary, there was no peace in Francesco's heart: for "who hath resisted God and hath had peace?"

We do not know in what circumstances, or by what influences his vocation now shaped itself before his mind under the austere form of the Passionist life. If there was anything abhorrent to his delicate nature, it was the thought of such a life. What little he then knew about it was from exaggerated public opinion, implying such a complete separation from the world, and such penances that his sensitive, pleasure-loving heart recoiled from it. In his difficulty of choosing between the institute of the Jesuits, for which he had been examined and approved, and that of the Passionists, of which he knew but little and perhaps cared less, he took the course dictated by prudence: he wrote to his director. This worthy clergyman, F. Peter Tedeschini, S. J., answered that a definite choice was to be made by his soul alone speaking to God alone; that it was an affair to be settled in prayers and tears rather than in any other way. "Have courage," said he, "keep ever in mind the thought of Jesus and Mary, and of the endless existence to which we are all hastening. And let these thoughts be fruitful of results: let them influence you strongly to overcome your passions; let them inspire you with hatred for sin, keep you from bad company, fill you with contempt for all vanity in conduct or attire, and make you trample under foot all human respect. Let these thoughts induce you to meditate on the eternal truths, and to receive the holy sacraments frequently: in a word, let them make you hate the world, its maxims and desires, and all that savors of it."

So, the meaning of it all was, that he should wait and pray. Of a certainty he prayed; as for waiting, nothing was more congenial to him just then, and by slow degrees, he fell back again into his sleep of worldliness.

The Possenti family had been considerably reduced in numbers since the death of their mother in 1842. Two of the children, Paul and Laurence, followed her within ten years, and two more left the parental roof shortly after; one (a daughter) to be a bride, the other (a son) to be a Dominican religious. Mary Louise, the eldest, remained at home devoting herself to her aged father, and with her four brothers, closed round him with all the greater affection as their numbers were decreasing. Old Pacifica still superintended the household with energy and devotedness; yet as Mary Louise grew up she came naturally to be looked upon as a mother by her much younger brothers. From his very infancy Francis had found in his sister all a mother's love and care; no one had greater influence over him, or was more willingly obeyed than she, and no two of the family understood each other better. Mary Louise had just passed her twenty-sixth birthday, when toward the close of May, 1855, the dread cholera having broken out in Spoleto, she fell as its first victim.

When the frightful scourge had passed, a reaction speedily set in throughout the city. Mourning and bereavement seemed to be forgotten: the theatre and the drawing-room were re-opened, and all sought to drown in gaiety their recent sorrows. Francesco was received in the families of his friends with sympathy and compassion: in manner he was reserved at first, then yielding to his buoyant spirits, and becoming interested in proportion to his success, he once more gave full rein to his passion for pleasure and worldly vanity. Through the great mercy of God, the final awakening for Francis took place shortly after, under the following circumstances.

In the cathedral of Spoleto there is venerated an ancient picture of the Mother of God, which on account of its eastern origin is called *Icon* or image. It was presented to the city by the Emperor Frederick Barbarossa, who sought thereby to conciliate the citizens after he had laid waste the surrounding country with fire and sword, in 1115. The emperor treasured the sacred image as an heirloom brought by his forefathers from Constantinople, and thus saved it from the senseless fury of the iconoclasts of the eighth century. It was accepted by the city as a sign of reconciliation and peace, and from that day, the merciful Mother rewarded the piety of her Spoletan clients, and the *Icon* became for them a fountain of graces. In the year 1856, however, a signal miracle excited to gratitude the faith of all, and made all her dear children of city and country flock to the cathedral to celebrate the festival of the Assumption with far more than customary pomp. During the cholera that decimated the city the Christian population had recourse to the Mother of Mercy: the sacred Icon was solemnly carried to the loggia (or balconied chamber overlooking the square in front of the cathedral) and the sorrow-stricken city was blessed with it. From that moment not a single new case of cholera was reported, and all those that were then sick were wonderfully cured.

On the octave day of the Assumption therefore, the titular of the cathedral, a solemn service of thanksgiving, was held in Spoleto, the concluding feature of which was a devout procession in which the miraculous Icon was carried.

With the grateful and enthusiastic multitude, our Francis repaired to the church, more through pious curiosity than any particular devotion, as he himself afterward acknowledged. Amidst the festive chant of the litany, the Icon was drawing near: Francis raised his eyes, and from her image, Mary cast upon him a glance that penetrated into his inmost heart, piercing it as with a dart of fire; at the same time, he heard a voice within his soul, a distinct interior locution, that said to him: "Why! thou art not made for the world!...What art thou doing in the world?...Hasten, become a religious!..."

No sound had struck the external air, the *Icon* passed by, and soon the echoes of the litany ceased, and the people dispersed to their homes, but the boy remained kneeling, his head bowed, his heart basking in the sunshine of interior peace. The victory was won! Such was the efficacy of that voice that it was forever enshrined in his memory, and as an additional proof of its celestial origin, from that moment a complete transformation came over his affections and inclinations; he had no thought, no desire, but that of following his vocation. When he realized the greatness of the favor accorded to him, giving way to his feelings, he burst into tears. Mary, who in the midst of his dangers had always protected him: Mary, by a miracle conquered all his repugnance, and changed his spirit of procrastination into determined resolution....He was to be a Passionist. On arriving home, the traces of his emotion were visible on his countenance, but he was more than usually cheerful: he had made up his mind, and peace was in his soul. At once he sought his confessor, F. Bompiani, S. J., who was likewise his instructor in philosophy, and the following is his account of what transpired. "I do not remember that Francis Possenti had ever manifested to me any inclination for the religious state; so quite unexpectedly, a certain Sunday afternoon in August, 1856, he asked for a private interview. He then candidly opened his heart concerning his intention of becoming a Passionist religious. I examined the matter thoroughly, both on account of its novelty and its strangeness (considering the boy's character). I cross-questioned him as to his motives, and made the most of the difficulties that he would encounter in the religious state of life. Our conversation in fact, lasted quite a while, but the signs of a real vocation were so unmistakable, that I advised him to notify his father of his intentions, and take the necessary steps to carry them into effect. At once he made formal application to the Provincial of the Passionists, including in his letter F. Bompiani's attestation of his moral character and proficiency in studies, and waited patiently (perhaps we should say impatiently) for a favorable reply. Meanwhile the scholastic year was drawing to its close, and the commencement was at hand. Francis determined that whether the reply to his application came before that day or not, it would be the utmost limit of his waiting. And it seems that he had grave reasons for not delaying, because as he afterward acknowledged to his spiritual director, he soon found out that had he tarried a single day longer, the world and the devil were preparing for him a snare of such a nature, that he might indeed have set his vocation aside; and that furthermore he was intimately convinced that our Lord would never have called him again."

But now came the painful task of acquainting his father with his resolution, and asking his consent and blessing. Summoning courage, and begging interiorly the divine assistance, one night, after the usual devotions of the household were over, he informed his father that he desired to speak to him in private. But no sooner were they alone, than Francis, overpowered by his feelings, burst into tears and sobs, unable for the moment to deal a blow that was so painful. Signor Possenti wondered at such an unlooked-for demonstration, and encouraged him to open his heart with freedom and all candor. When Francis could trust himself to speak, he said, "Father, I have made up my mind to become a religious, and I desire your consent and blessing." On hearing such a declaration, Signor Possenti could hardly refrain from laughing outright. "You want to be a religious, my son?...why," said he, smiling, "your life has been one of vanity and pleasure....How would you wear a rough cassock, you who have always been so particular about your clothes? Then see, my dear boy, your vocation is nothing but a sudden notion: no sooner has the fancy struck you, than you want to run off somewhere or other, and then perhaps come back in disgrace. My son, that will never do: you must take time, and discuss the matter with your director. If you have a real vocation, time will tell." But Francis foresaw these objections, and was well prepared to answer them.

"Father," said he, "you are mistaken in supposing that my desire to enter the religious state is grounded on a sudden fancy: I have thought it over for a long while: in fact, I had a lengthy interview with my spiritual director. At first he spoke to me just like you, but at last he expressed himself fully satisfied: and it is with his approval that I broach the subject to you: he told me to do it. Besides, father, fearing my own weakness and procrastination, I have already made application to the Provincial of the Passionists to be received amongst them."

Here was a double surprise for the good man. That his son should wish to become a religious was serious enough, but what about becoming a Passionist? "My son," said he, "what do you know about those religious? Have you any idea how hard their rule is?" And then the afflicted father with all the affection of his heart backed by the subtlety of the practiced lawyer, began to represent all the difficulties that he could think of, if not to disabuse his son of his resolution, at least to gain time. But Francis threw himself at his father's feet, assuring him that he would not arise until his consent was granted. Signor Possenti knew not what to do: it seemed utterly useless to try to make his son relinquish his desire: to yield at once might be imprudent. At last, wishing to effect a compromise, he told his son that while he could not refuse him conscientiously, still he was not quite prepared to give his approval unreservedly: he assured him that he would consider the matter at once, and would tell him of his decision later.

When Francis had retired, who can describe the perplexities of his father's heart? Did God really ask for the sacrifice? He had already given to religion his eldest son Aloysius, who joined the Dominicans; another son, Henry, had just entered the seminary to study for the priesthood; two more of his sons had died within a few years, in the flower of their young manhood; his two daughters had left him, Teresa to follow her husband to a distant city, and Mary Louise, the sweet angel of the home, for heaven....He was now sixty-six years old....Should he be left alone now that the infirmities of age were coming upon him?...He had looked up to Francis, the brightest and most amiable of his remaining children, as the stay of his declining years and the glory of the family....Could he live without this well-loved son, or permit him to shut himself up in a poor Passionist monastery?...Yet he was a Christian, a man of faith. It might break his heart to lead this child of his love to the mountain of sacrifice, but if God so commanded, he would obey....

Two persons principally were to help the prudent father to come to an enlightened decision, his own son Aloysius, a Dominican, who was then on a visit to his family, and the Vicar-General of Loretto, F. Caesar Acquacotta, a man of piety and learning, and an old friend of Signor Possenti.

Francis had no great difficulty in winning over his brother to his side. Aloysius reported favorably to his father, and that same evening the general arrangements for departure were agreed upon. Father Aloysius on the way back to his religious home had to pass through Loretto, and after visiting the sacred shrine of Our Lady, they were to call on F. Acquacotta. Francesco was to present a letter from his father to the vicar asking the latter as an old friend of the family, to examine the boy's vocation, and authorizing him to give in Signor Possenti's name, the necessary approval and consent. Furthermore as a last resort to test his son's vocation, it was agreed that from Loretto a visit should be made to Morrovalle, not far distant, where the Passionist novitiate was situated. Perhaps, thought the prudent parent, a visit to the lonely monastery might have more effect than all other arguments combined, and divest his son's resolution of the glamour of poetry and enthusiasm, when standing face to face with the uninviting reality.

Francis was well satisfied with such a plan, in fact nothing could have pleased him better; for in his sincere determination, he felt proof against any persuasion or hindrance whatsoever. The next morning he was found kneeling in gratitude before the image of Our Lady of Sorrows in the church of the

Servite Fathers. This day, the 5th of September, 1856, was the last day he was to spend in the world as a secular; it was likewise the date of the "commencement" exercises at the Jesuit College. The audience assembled in the spacious hall, and was composed of the most brilliant society of the city. Monsignor Guadalupi, the Apostolic Delegate, presided, supported by the Archbishop of Spoleto on the one side, and Signor Possenti, the chief magistrate, on the other. It was a day of triumph for our Francis. He had been selected to deliver the introductory discourse, for he was confessedly without a rival not only in gracefulness of person and carriage, but especially in oratorical excellence. His friend, Bonaccia, describes him very minutely as he stood on the stage on that memorable occasion. "His clothes," he says, "were unusually elegant; a matchless and richly-folded shirt front adorned with jewels; bright buttons on his cuffs; a silk cravat around his neck; his hair studiously parted: add to this picture, his white kid gloves and patent leather shoes, and we have a pen-picture of young Francis Possenti as he stood smiling and serene, facing his many friends and the distinguished audience, about to be the pleased spectators of his triumphs. I have always felt," continues his friend and biographer, "that Francesco thus appeared in all the vain ornaments of the world, to bid his farewell to it forever, and to show how poorly he esteemed such baubles by turning his back upon them, at the very moment when he was the recipient of so many honors and so much applause. At the end of the exercises, when Francis was called before the Delegate to receive the gold medal for excellence in all his studies, the whole assembly testified its joy, and Signor Possenti was voted the happiest of fathers in having such a distinguished son, the Apostolic Delegate himself publicly congratulating him in the warmest terms....But alas, poor father....He alone knew his son's secret; and the more he witnessed and realized his son's merit, the more keenly did he feel his own impending loss."

On reaching home, after bidding good-bye to his many friends, who all imagined that he was merely going to spend his vacation in the country, Francis found the household in commotion. At the last moment the news had been told by the afflicted parent. The morning of that day had dawned on the brightest hopes, its noon had shone on congratulations and glory, but it closed in tears.

The great news could not remain a secret. The next morning it spread among the students, and surprise was visible on every face. Toward the close of the scholastic course, the choice of a state of life is generally a topic of conversation in a college. That particular year, the Passionists were spoken of, for two of the collegians had left for the novitiate shortly before; but when a third candidate was mentioned, and that one Francis Possenti, it was like a thunderbolt from a clear sky. Whatever may have been their opinions, and they were various, all felt sincerely sorry to lose their talented companion, whom all loved for his excellent qualities and kind disposition. But when they found out their loss, Francesco was already miles on the road to the cloister.

5 His Journey to the Novitiate

"A man's enemies shall be they of his own household."

Francis bade adieu to his good father and brothers, and set out for Loretto with his brother F. Aloysius, on September 6th, 1856, arriving at the holy shrine on the evening of the day following. Next to Jerusalem and Bethlehem, there is perhaps no pilgrimage dearer to the heart of Mary's children or frequented in greater numbers, than the *Santa Casa*, or Holy House. Loretto now possesses this inestimable treasure. This is the very dwelling wherein our Blessed Mother was born, in which Gabriel, the angel of the Lord declared unto Mary and she conceived by the Holy Ghost, the identical house in which "the Word was made flesh and dwelt among us"; the house that in 1291 was carried by angel-hands from Nazareth to Dalmatia, to save it from the fanatical Turks, and was transported once more from Dalmatia, over the Adriatic sea to the laurel-fields, Loretto, where it is now venerated.

Our travelers arrived in the city after the Holy House was closed; "but the next morning at daybreak," F. Aloysius says, "in spite of the fatigue of our journey, my brother was already in the church, where he remained in prayer until after eight o'clock, the hour appointed to meet our uncle, the Vicar-General, Canon Acquacotta. He received us with the greatest cordiality, and insisted on our remaining till the morrow. After a brief interview, his duties called him away, and we all repaired to the church to assist at the solemn office and mass, that being the festival of Our Lady's nativity. At the conclusion of dinner, my uncle called us apart, and he then undertook the task of examining my brother's vocation, and changing his resolution of joining the Passionists."

This was to be the first of the last three battles which tried our hero's constancy, and all three came from his relations: so true is it that "a man's enemies will be those of his own household." The canon commenced by alleging all the arguments he could think of, attacking the boy's vocation from every quarter: he placed before him forcibly the difficulties with which he would have to contend, and the weakness of human nature in general, to say nothing of Gabriel's delicate constitution in particular, when measured against such an austere rule. "Who better than I," said he, "ought to know what kind of a life they lead? I was amongst them myself during the troubles of 1848, and I assure you, I still remember with painful clearness the hardships of the Passionist observance: and you, my dear nephew, without any experience, brought up in the midst of plenty, with no strength to boast of either, want to join them! How on earth will you be able to stand the strain by night as well as by day? My dear boy," he concluded, "don't allow yourself to be deceived by a sudden fit of fervor. This matter is a little too serious for you to run any unnecessary risks. Don't be in such a hurry: take plenty of time and think over it; but of course, if you are wedded to your own opinion, and come to find your mistake later on, remember that you'll have nobody to blame but yourself."

Simply, but very earnestly, Francis replied to his uncle's reasoning, by assuring him that there could be no fair doubt entertained of his religious vocation. Then he proceeded to explain in the greatest detail, the history of his call to a higher life: that so far from its being a sudden whim, originating in his imagination, on the contrary, it was a grace against which he had been struggling for years, and that nothing short of the firmest conviction that it was God's will for him to be a religious, induced him to obey;—and as far as the Congregation of the Passionists was concerned, their austerities were certainly not more than their rule enjoined; and if some of his companions succeeded, why shouldn't he?— and finally as to health, God would not have called him to such an order, unless He intended to help him according to his need.

Now, the canon being an enlightened and holy man, saw in the speech and manner of the boy before him, all the signs of a true vocation. He at once wrote the result of this examination to Signor Possenti. Meanwhile he encouraged Francis to be faithful, and to walk steadfastly in the arduous path which he had chosen. Instead of sharing in the festivities in honor of the day, which were to take place in the public square, Francis preferred to spend the whole evening in the church, pouring forth his soul in thanksgiving to God, and asking for the protection of the Virgin-Mother. He next made a general confession of his whole life, and received Holy Communion the ensuing morning at the altar of the Holy House, and set out with his brother for the Passionist novitiate. On their way they tarried for a while at the home of their mother's parents. Right welcome they were indeed, and the most cordial hospitality was tendered them: but no sooner had they heard of Francesco's intentions than everything changed very unpleasantly. He at once became the object of the unfavorable remarks and stinging jests of the whole family. Everyone seemed to have the right to interpret his conduct, and to pester him with uncalled-for advice. "Why should he give up the brilliant prospects of life?...Why couldn't he save his soul as a good secular?...Why couldn't he remain outside the cloister, and edify the world like his good father?...At least,—if he wanted to become a secular priest, all right...but for him to bury himself in a monastery, and what was worse, to join the Passionists...why, the very idea was silly....He ought to have better sense....Was it right for such a clever son to break his father's heart by leaving home?...Was that all his poor father deserved from him, for all that he had done for his son's welfare?..."

What could our Francis say?...It is a hard thing to be misunderstood by those whom we love, it is distressing to be derided by those whom we reverence. The warmth of their welcome was chilled by the sadness of parting. In their judgment, the boy was stubborn, he was obstinate; but they knew right well that he would soon be sorry, and retrace his steps!—Of a truth, "a man's enemies shall be they of his own household."

Toward evening the two brothers having resumed their journey, arrived at Morrovalle, their journey's end. There was in the town itself a Capuchin monastery, the superior of which was the uncle of our travelers, so they determined to call upon him. Here again Francis had to stand his ground, for his zealous uncle seemed to doubt the genuineness of the young man's vocation. The battle of Loretto had to be fought over again. "Look here," said F. John Baptist, "look at this poor tunic of mine: isn't it rough enough for anybody? Well, I tell you that the habit worn by those Passionist Fathers is yet worse."

But all in vain: with the same simplicity and firmness with which he pleaded his cause before the Vicar-General, Francis answered the guardian's objections. God had clearly shown that He called him to that state of life, and he was resolved to trust to God's grace and mercy. The good superior listened patiently to the young man, and he was not only satisfied with his arguments, but with the straightforwardness of an unselfish soul, he actually rejoiced at being vanquished, and promised moreover to introduce him the next morning to the Master of Novices, who was the friar's personal friend.

On the morning, then, of the 10th of September, 1856, Francis, with his two companions, walked to the retreat of the Passionists, three miles outside of the city....O blessed congregation which was about to receive so great a treasure!—the worthy offspring of pious Christian parents, educated by the sons of La Salle and Loyola, bedewed with grace in the sanctuary of the Servites of Mary,—it belonged to the sons of Dominic and Francis to plant with their own hands in the humble garden of the Passion, this predestined soul, this blessed seed that was to bring forth such flowers of virtue and fruits of holiness, the glory of which belongs to them all. But who can describe the joy of Francis himself, when for the first time he rested his eyes on the blessed retreat that was to separate him from the world, to bring peace to his soul and unite him to his God? The boy's heart leaped for joy when he stood on the threshold of the cloister, and saw the doors of the monastery opening for him.

And yet, he was not without apprehension. Would he be received?...No answer had reached him from the F. Provincial, to whom he had written asking for admission....If not expected, would he be allowed to remain?...Such were his reflections as the company waited in the plain parlor. But the cheerful appearance of the Master of Novices dispelled his misgivings: he *was* expected. A favorable answer had been sent, but Signor Possenti probably judged it better to keep the letter. On the other hand, when the Provincial heard nothing further from the young candidate, and fearing lest his letter went astray, he wrote a second time, reaffirming his acceptance and urging Francis to solicit his father's consent, and start at once. This last letter, however, reached Spoleto only after the two brothers were on their journey to Loretto and Morrovalle, leaving them in a state of great uneasiness, under the circumstances. There was just one vacancy at the time in the novitiate, and the postulant was entrusted to the care of the Vice-Master, who introduced Francis to his new companions. He was safe at last!—he found himself in the midst of the children of the Passion! The sight of the religious habit, the peaceful oratory, the solitary cells, the simple piety and joyful mirth depicted on every face:—all made him feel happy, for among his new-found brethren he was at home.

It had been arranged by their uncle, that this should be only a preliminary visit, and that Francis should return to the Capuchin convent, and go thence on a visit to Montegiorgio, where his aunt lived; but when he found himself secure in the harbor of religion, it was useless to expect him to launch his bark anew on the troubled waves of the secular world. He gently refused to leave the retreat. He might have a chance, said he, to visit those relatives some other time, but it was plainly out of the question for him just then. "The next morning when I called," says his brother Aloysius, "I found him more than happy. He requested me to make known his contentment to our father also: and thus, we bade one another farewell."

6 Life in the Novitiate

It is customary that a postulant before being admitted to take the religious habit, shall live in his secular dress in company with our brethren for some time, according to the prudence and determination of the superiors and seniors of the novitiate, that his suitableness may be gauged by a preliminary trial. Afterward, he devoted himself during ten days to sacred exercises and pious meditations, that being thereby more and more enlightened and united with God, he may be better prepared to make the sacrifice of himself. Two of his fellow-students from the college had preceded Francis by a few days and were to be admitted to vestition on the third Sunday of September, and to his great delight, Francis, having made his formal petition before the fathers of the local Chapter, was allowed to commence his spiritual retreat with his old friends, the next day after his arrival.

On receiving the religious habit, the candidate changes his name, a usage common to many ancient orders, and which we find mentioned frequently in the Scriptures. The fact of imposing a name is indicative of authority over the person thus called, whilst for him it is symbolic of the advice of the Holy Ghost "to put off, according to your former conversation, the old man who is corrupted according to the desire of error; and be renewed in the spirit of your mind, and put on the new man, who, according to God, is created in justice and holiness of truth." Furthermore, there is added to the new name a title, reminding the novice of some special devotion. Thus, in

Passionist Novitiate, Morrovalle

the case before us, Francesco Possenti became known to his brethren at home, and the Christian world abroad, as Brother, (or as we call it) *Confrater*[7] *Gabriel* of the Sorrowful Virgin. By this name, therefore, will he be called henceforward, and we shall see how fully it was justified and illustrated in the whole tenor of his religious life.

As the days of his retreat of preparation went on, the Holy Spirit kindled in the heart of the postulant a fervor, of which we may judge from the following incident, and which will likewise explain why the capitular fathers reduced to its minimum the time of the preliminary probation.

In our novitiate the novices frequently give an account of their meditation. Now it happened, as F. Norbert, the Vice-Master relates, "that on one of the few days before Gabriel's vestition, there came over to Morrovalle on a day's recreation the students of the neighboring retreat of Recanati, with their director. The latter passing by the chapter-room of the novices, whilst they were giving an account of their prayer, chanced to overhear a few words that struck him; and yielding to curiosity, he stopped and listened to what was being said at the gathering of the novices. Now, the sentiments, reflections and applications were such that they made an extraordinary impression upon his mind. When he called on the master, he inquired who the novice was that had given an account of his prayer: and great was his wonder on learning that it was a

---

[7] Editor's Note: This title was used to distinguish those preparing for the priesthood, such as St. Gabriel, from the lay brothers, who were called "Frater," meaning "Brother."

young man who had arrived in the monastery only a few days before."

What the day of his betrothal is to a youthful lover, such to the future religious is the day on which he is betrothed to the religious institute of his choice. For him it is truly "the day of the joy of his heart." This joy can be realized fully only by those who have actually experienced its ineffable consolations; but it is not difficult to surmise that these consolations must have been particularly intense in a soul so well prepared by the Holy Ghost, as was that of our dear Gabriel. During the ceremony of receiving the habit, his tears could not escape the notice of his companions; that same evening too he wept, when according to custom, he knelt in the refectory, and publicly thanked the community for having received him into the congregation.

He wrote at once to his father and brothers at home about this great event, and the depths to which his soul was stirred are evident in every line of his letter. It runs as follows:

Morrovalle, Sept. 21st, 1856

My dear Father:—The day has come at last. The Almighty had been calling me for a long time, whilst I ungratefully turned a deaf ear to His voice, by enjoying the world and displeasing Him; but His infinite mercy sweetly disposed all things, and to-day the feast of Our Lady of Sorrows, our Mother and Protector, I was clothed in the holy habit, taking the name of Confrater Gabriel, of the Seven Dolors.

Up to the present, my dear father, I have not experienced anything but pleasure, whether as regards this religious congregation, or my vocation to it. Oh, rest assured that whosoever is called to the religious state receives a grace that he will never be able fully to comprehend!

My excellent F. Master and Vice-Master send their kind regards together with my own. My greetings to the Jesuits and Oratorians, as well as to all enquiring friends.

Begging your blessing, dearest Father,

I remain your affectionate son,

Confrater Gabriel,

Of the Dolors of Mary, Passionist.

This was his first letter to his family and friends: this was the first time that he could publicly style himself a Passionist, and call himself by his new name. He gloried in being a Knight of Jesus Crucified, and never did maiden delight in elegant finery, or prince in gold-embroidered robe, as did Gabriel in the livery of the Passion that he wore. Often did he assert that he would not exchange his poor, rough tunic for a royal mantle; daily would he kiss his habit with unspeakable devotion.

Still, "the habit does not make the monk." By its modest singularity, the religious garb is emblematic of separation from the world, not necessarily in body, but in customs, principles, and conduct—that is in spirit. Is it not evident that the love of God, and the love of "the things which are in the world" cannot coexist in the same heart? No man can serve two masters. The attempt to effect a compromise between them, was as we have seen, the error and the danger of this servant of

God in his secular days, until the grace of God triumphed at last, and set him free. That such a victory should be the fruit of arduous combat and prayer, is the ordinary rule of the supernatural life; but that it should be brought about as it were instantaneously is indeed a wonder. Such a remarkable phenomenon, however, we have now to consider, and in Gabriel's own words, it may be aptly styled "his conversion." Hitherto he had loved the world as far as was compatible with the state of grace, but no sooner did he enter the cloister than he could say with Christ's apostle "The world is crucified to me, and I to the world."

The first great marvel in the life of our hero, is his perfect aversion to the world, and everything belonging to it. Such a transformation was effected simply by the predilection of God for this chosen soul, to whom He imparted the spirit of his vocation not gradually and by installments, but rather in its fullness, from the very beginning of his religious life. All at once, he was a changed man, with a new mind, a new heart, new desires, new affections: grace had suddenly conquered and transformed nature. It would sometimes happen that the conversation of his companions would innocently turn on some secular topics: on such occasions Confrater Gabriel would dexterously strive to divert it into different channels; and should this prove impracticable, then would he pass such subjects over as lightly and as quickly as possible. In one word then, from the day of his receiving the holy habit, Gabriel put on the new man, and of his former self there was absolutely no trace left. Against the pleasures of the world, of which he had been so fond, he now conceived a hatred that vented itself in his correspondence. He thus writes to one of his old-time companions: "My dearest friend: You are right in saying that the world is full of stumbling-blocks, and that it is a very hard thing to save one's soul in it; yet you must not give up courage, for even in the secular world it is not impossible to become holy.

"Dear Philip, if you truly love your soul, shun evil companions; shun the theatre. I know by experience how very difficult it is while entering such places in the state of grace, to come away without either having lost it, or at least exposed it to great danger. Shun pleasure-parties, and shun evil books. I assure you that if I had remained in the world, it seems certain to me that I would not have saved my soul. Tell me, could anyone have indulged in more amusements than I? Well, and what is the result?—nothing but bitterness and fear.

"Dear Philip, do not despise me, for it is my heart that speaks. I ask your pardon for all the scandal that I may have given you; and I protest that whatever evil I may have spoken about anyone, I now unsay it, and beg of you to forget it all, and to pray for me that God may forgive me likewise."

That our Gabriel was more than exaggerated in self-condemnation, can easily be gathered from the preceding chapters; his friends were unanimous in asserting that nothing seriously reprehensible was ever seen in his conduct; the companions to whom he alludes, were such as may be met with even in some of our best colleges; the entertainments to which he refers, would be considered as select from an ordinary standpoint; the theatres of the Pontifical States were not as licentious as the best in this country; the romances of which he speaks would be deemed choice literature, when judged by the standards set up by our newspapers, magazines and cheap novels.

Instead of decreasing, Gabriel's aversion for the pleasures of the world went on increasing in proportion as he became more enlightened from on high. A few weeks before his precious death, when already in the dawn of that light that never faileth, he wrote these words in his last letter to his father: "I do naught but bless the merciful hand of the Blessed Virgin that rescued me from the world." These strong words need not surprise anyone who remembers the language of St. John the evangelist: "I write to you, young men, because you are strong, and the word of God abideth in you, and you have overcome the wicked one. Love not the world, nor the things that are in the world. If any man love the world, the charity of the Father is not in him: for all that is in the world is the concupiscence of the flesh, and the concupiscence of the eyes, and the pride of life, which is not of the Father, but is of the world. And the world passeth away, and the concupiscence thereof; but he that doeth the will of God, abideth forever." (1 John 2:14-17)

But if Christ demands separation from the world in all His disciples, He requires something more perfect from those who wish to follow Him closely. To those only who abandon house and brethren, and sisters, father, mother and children and lands for His sake, does He promise the hundredfold here below, and life everlasting afterward. He alone, who has made this sacrifice, can tell how difficult it is: a sacrifice all the more painful as it immolates for the sake of divine love, affections which of themselves are perfectly legitimate: all the more heroic, as it is only a counsel, there being no law that absolutely exacts it. The memories of our native land and home, of former friends and associations are deeply embedded in our hearts by the hand of nature: but from the day Gabriel set his foot in the cloister, he showed himself so completely detached from all such things, that he never brought them up as topics for conversation, except on rare occasions, and then only for the sake of some edifying reflection.

The letters he received from home, he would never unseal, even with the permission of his superior; he would not even take them into his hands nor read them, unless obedience obliged him to do so. "Do you assure me," he would say, "that I will not have to answer to God for this?" So that, as a rule, his superiors had to read his letters for him; and even then, Gabriel would ask them to tell him only what was necessary and to the point, passing over everything else. In the beginning he showed an extreme aversion to correspond with anyone; so much so, that the Father Master of the novitiate judging this tendency to be exaggerated and excessive, had to urge him from time to time to write to his family. In this however it was with difficulty that he prevailed over Gabriel's reluctance. The novice would frequently show how distasteful letter-writing was to him by asking questions like these: "Father, do the others write to their parents?...Do you take upon yourself in this matter, whatever violation of the rule there may be?..."

The fervent young man however, soon came to know and understand better the wisdom and prudence of his rule, and with a docile mind he obeyed it; for, although "the writing of frequent and unnecessary letters to relatives" is not encouraged, still the religious "are recommended to follow, as a general rule, the custom of the congregation, namely of writing home three or four times a year."

This, however, could not satisfy Signor Possenti: hence, a month had hardly elapsed since his son had been clothed in the Passionist habit, when the novice had to answer the gentle remonstrances of his anxious and affectionate father. "My dear father," he wrote, "you tell me that I ought to write twice a month, but this is impossible: still F. Master bids me inform you that over and above the ordinary times, he will not fail to allow me to write if I ever stand in need of anything, or have any special communication to make. For the rest, be assured that I am very well, and will not fail to avail myself of the above permission whenever necessary." This last assurance, however, had to be renewed more than once to his over-anxious parent.

More jealous still was our young novice to avoid visits that would have brought him back to a world, from which he was so glad to escape. He did not wish his solitude to be broken in upon by seculars, whether relatives or friends. The reader may recollect that on account of Gabriel's eagerness to enter the novitiate, a visit to his relatives in the neighboring city of Montegiorgio was deferred. No sooner had the ensuing spring arrived, than his uncle wrote to Signor Possenti informing him that they were organizing a large party to call on Gabriel at his retreat in Morrovalle, thinking no doubt, that the young religious would enjoy "a day off" just as much as they. But no sooner did the fervent novice hear of this, than he overcame his dislike for letter-writing, and at once begged his father to make them postpone their visit until after his profession; and with great delicacy he added: "Let not the thought cross your mind that I have been influenced or even advised by my superiors in this matter. Indeed, they would show themselves indifferent about such things, and would put no obstacle in my way. Pardon me, dear father, and kindly comply with my wishes." His friends showed themselves quite reasonable; they only changed their plans, but they did not give them up. They took him at his word and when his term of noviceship was over, they prepared a great reception for him at their own home. When Gabriel learned this, he wrote thus to his father: "In your last letter you spoke of the proposed outing to Montegiorgio, the time having now arrived when it might be allowed. But, my dear father, shall I speak to you frankly? Well, then, let me tell you that I see no necessity at all for such a visit: and not only this, but I deem it incompatible with my present state of life and not at all conducive to my spiritual welfare. Besides, such visits are not customary among Passionists. How then could I, only just professed, dare to ask my superiors for a privilege which the senior religious do not request? Still, if I have to pass through that city (and it is likely enough, since we are about to open a retreat hard by) then, I may avail myself of the opportunity, and permission will not be refused." His friends were as edified as they were disappointed by this letter, and in face of his fervent earnestness they gracefully submitted. A few months after his profession he was transferred to Pievetorina, where he was visited by his brother Michael, and good old Pacifica. On all such occasions, he showed himself extremely courteous, affable and cheerful, but as soon as politeness would allow, or the observance bell summoned him to some community exercise, he at once took leave of his visitors. Once only, during his year of probation, did obedience bring him into the midst of his relatives. The legal settlement of certain family affairs was to take place at Fermo, not far distant from Montegiorgio. "I was the one who accompanied him," writes F. Norbert, his Vice-Master. "He met his sister Teresa in the office, and held converse with her for some time declaring his content of mind and happiness, discoursing on spiritual matters quite unaffectedly. What he said to her, I of course do not know, but I remember that she seemed very much impressed and edified." "Although we had not met for a long time," she writes herself in the processes, "my brother never spoke to me until his superior gave him permission." "We took occasion of our presence in Fermo," F. Norbert continues, "to pay a visit to the college of the Jesuit Fathers, with some of whom, especially F. Cardella, and F. Rossi the rector, Confrater Gabriel was well acquainted. The latter took me aside and asked: 'How does this young man conduct himself?...' 'Very well indeed,' I answered. 'But,' insisted F. Rossi, 'he used to be somewhat giddy.' 'The grace of his vocation has remedied that,' I replied. 'He is a youth of strong purpose, as fervent and virtuous as can be desired, and if he so continues, as we have every reason to hope, he will really *become a saint*.'"

7 His Affections Spiritualized

In joining the religious state, no one is required to suppress his God-given nature; or to smother the affections of his heart; all that Christ asks from a religious is that he spiritualize and purify his love: that he disengage his affections from all that is merely sensible and selfish. There are now extant some twenty-six letters written by Confrater Gabriel, during the six years he spent in religion, and the greater number were addressed to his father and brothers at home. Written though they were off-hand, and devoid of any special claim to literary excellence, they nevertheless reveal in all their naturalness and beauty, the sentiments of a soul purged of every worldly attachment, in which every affection is transformed by the love of God poured forth in the heart by the grace of the Holy Ghost. They are replete with counsels of heavenly wisdom, given with such effusive candor and warmth that one cannot help feeling that they come from a loving heart. He took the keenest interest in every event that occurred in his family, but from a higher standpoint than worldly considerations could inspire. His father lays before him certain plans regarding himself and his brothers: Gabriel writes at once: "I see no objection to your taking up your residence in Rome; all-the-less since my three brothers may there exercise their profession under your eyes. But you ought to find out whether the air of Rome would agree with you; although as far as the summer heat is concerned, you could find plenty of places in the neighborhood to which you might retire. You do not ask me anything about Vincent's state of life, nor do I dare obtrude my advice thereupon: only, I beg you not to place earthly interests on a par with those of his soul, for 'what doth it profit a man if he gain the whole world and lose his own soul': 'only one thing is necessary.'"

His cousin, Peter Possenti, is laboring under a severe affliction: Gabriel hastens to comfort him in his bereavement. "I am very sorry," he writes, "to hear from my father (whose grief is as great as mine) of the death of your good wife and her newborn daughter. Faith teaches us to submit to the will of God, who permits all things for our good. Doubtless the shock must have been painful, but what shall we do? Shall we allow these distressing events to pass by without deriving wholesome spiritual profit? Oh, no! Though we cannot help feeling the blow, let us not be overcome by our sorrow. Let us turn to the Lord, and offer up our sacrifice with courage. I will not fail to pray for the repose of her soul, although I trust that she has already received the reward of her many virtues." True Christian charity weeps with them that mourn; but it rejoices, too, with them that are in joy. Gabriel's father retires from public life; his son congratulates him thereupon in the following terms: "I give thanks to the Lord for sparing you to celebrate your jubilee. You have no intrigues now to fear any more, and will have more leisure to turn your attention to the principal end of man's existence here upon earth; for, after the short labor of a few days, we expect from an almighty and generous Master, peace and eternal jubilee. May our Blessed Mother be your special advocate, and thank our God in the name of us all for all the favors granted to you."

In every letter that he wrote, he humbly asks his friends and family for their prayers, and assures them of his own. Blessed be the family that has a representative before the throne of grace! The annual recurrence of the great church festivals always gave him an opportunity to pour out the feelings of his heart. This is one of his Easter greetings: "My sincere love for you, my dearest father, prompts me to fulfill my duty both as a Christian and as your child. May then Jesus and Mary themselves cause these paschal festivities to be a source of joy for you and all at home, and all my relatives: and this wish of mine comes more from my heart than from my lips. God knows that I speak the truth." The feast of Pentecost inspires him with the following lines: "May the eternal and divine Spirit come down upon you and my brothers during these days, and bring you that spirit of truth, of consolation and of peace, which is a pledge of eternal salvation: and may our most loving Mother Mary, who is all kindness and compassion, repay you for the great care and solicitude you have always shown for our welfare and education." But it was at Christmas-tide especially that this loving son revealed the affections of his heart. "My dearest Father,...since we have already entered upon the advent season, I wish to anticipate my duty in wishing you, and my brothers, and all at home, the sweetest and holiest joys and blessings of the coming Christmas. Let us pray to the infant Jesus, who came down into a vile and cold stable, to deliver us from the eternal punishment which our sins deserved. Let us ask of Him to purify our hearts by a good, holy communion, and inflame them with His divine love."

"The recurrence of Christmas," he writes the following year, "invites all the faithful to wish one another those blessings of which our Saviour is both the author and dispenser. Now if such be the custom between neighbors and friends, what should be the sentiments of a loving son to his affectionate father? I will not expatiate in vain compliments, but I sincerely pray that my desires for yourself and all at home be heard by the divine Infant and His amiable Mother." Again, the following year: "The season of peace, mercy and grace is drawing near, and I feel it my duty to wish from my inmost heart, to you and all at home, a season full of God's blessings, a season of true gladness that will long live in your memories. Yes, dearest father, brothers and all, may Jesus be born in your hearts; may Mary always guard Him there; may Joseph, the holy angels and the childlike shepherds keep Him company and intercede for us. What more can I wish for you, than that this holy family take you under their protection?"

The worldling may perhaps smile at such epistolary expressions; but "My thoughts are not your thoughts, nor your ways My ways," saith the Lord. In vain will one look in Gabriel's letters for anything newsy, or interesting from a mere secular point of view: he was dead to all mundane concerns, but the affections of his heart in being thus purified from earthly dross, became all the more ardent and lasting; those who were dear to him appreciated and reciprocated his affection, and evidenced it by the eagerness with which they longed for his letters, and by the religious care with which they preserved them.

8 His Clerical Studies

When the year of his novitiate was ended, Gabriel pronounced his vows before the whole religious community. This happy event took place on Tuesday, September 22nd, 1857. It is easier to experience than to describe the joy and consolation of one's religious profession: and "to attempt to do anything like justice, in describing Confrater Gabriel's profession, would as F. Germanus[8] writes, be quite impossible. A year before, at the foot of the same altar, during the ceremony of his vestition, he had not been able to contain his tears of consolation; but now, during the ceremony of profession, he was well-nigh overcome by the vehemence of his affections. His countenance was inflamed, and his whole appearance resembled that of an earthly seraph." The Sunday after his consecration, he wrote thus to his father: "Through the grace of God, and the protection of Our Lady of Sorrows, and to my unspeakable joy, my desires have been fulfilled, and I have made my holy profession. Such a grace can never be valued adequately, and therefore as I have been favored by Almighty God with such a privilege, I feel bound by an ever-increasing obligation to correspond thereto. I leave it therefore to your own judgment, whether or no I stand in need of the prayers of yourself and others."

---

[8] Editor's Note: Father Germanus Ruoppolo, C.P., has been declared Venerable by the Church. In addition to being the postulator of the cause of St. Gabriel's canonization, he was also the spiritual director of St. Gemma Galgani.

Gabriel was destined to commence his professional clerical studies in the retreat of Pievetorina, but had to wait in the novitiate for the profession of some of his future companions. During these five months he and his two associates attended to their studies privately under the guidance of F. Norbert, his former Vice-Master who had been appointed the director and lector of the new class. Pievetorina is a lovely little town of the Marches, and one of the most important of the district of Camerino: it lies along the course of the river Chienti, in the midst of a plain surrounded on all sides by woods and hills.

It has ever been customary in our congregation to scatter the regular students among the retreats which form our provinces, and the constant union of senior and junior religious in the common observance, has proved of mutual assistance and edification, while the occasional change of scenery and surroundings, consequent upon their removal from one retreat to another, helps to maintain the young men in a healthy condition of body and mind. So it came to pass that after having spent nearly a year and a-half in Pievetorina, F. Norbert's class was transferred to another monastery, situated in the kingdom of Naples. The students lost nothing by the change, for the new retreat is surrounded by the loftiest mountains, and has the advantage of the healthiest and most bracing air. Tradition has it that the monastery now occupied by the sons of St. Paul of the Cross was founded by the seraphic Father St. Francis. He established here a family of his sons who, under the patronage of the Immaculate Virgin, served and praised God in these sacred precincts till the end of the last century, when the sectaries of the French revolution scattered all the religious orders of the kingdom of Naples. No place could have been desired more appropriate for a Passionist retreat, being situated about two miles and a-half from the town. Here it was that Confrater Gabriel passed the last years of his short life, and though the greater number of the religious who had known him were dead, yet, when the processes for his canonization were introduced, by a special providence of God, the few who survived were of such a character, as to give peculiar weight to their testimony. By far the most important of these was F. Norbert of St. Mary, who though comparatively young in years, when he was first entrusted with Gabriel's direction, showed himself fully worthy of the confidence placed in him by the higher superiors. In his deposition he speaks as follows: "I became acquainted with Gabriel on the day he entered the novitiate, and from that moment we never parted until death separated us. He constantly lived under my authority: before his profession I was his Vice-Master, afterward I became his lector and spiritual director. Only a few times during my absence did he confess to any other religious, and I do not think that he ever had a spiritual conference with anybody else. I have therefore been the eyewitness of his whole life, was entrusted with all the secrets of his heart, knew all that passed in his mind, was informed of all the dispositions and occupations of his beautiful soul: nothing was hidden from me." God so disposed that when the cause was introduced at Rome there still survived Gabriel some of his former friends and companions, who could testify concerning every portion of his life in the world as a secular, as well as every phase of his religious career, so "that in the mouth of two or three witnesses every word may stand."

In the scholasticate, there begins for the young Passionist cleric the second period of his religious life, which is a gradual and progressive preparation for the special ministry of his vocation. This preparation is necessarily of a twofold nature, that of the mind and heart: the former must be furnished with knowledge, the latter must be inured to the practice of solid virtue. One's fitness and willingness for the religious state, has been tested and gauged in the novitiate, and he has been fairly started in his career as a Passionist. What the cleric now needs is less a master to teach him the simple theory of this spiritual science, than a director to guide his still uncertain steps in its difficult practice. Hand in hand with his growth in holiness is his advance in ecclesiastical learning under the leadership of his professor or lector, so that the future missionary, "the man of God," as the apostle says (2 Timothy 3:17), "may be perfect, furnished unto every good work." It is not what he reads in a book, or hears in a lecture-room that will fit a priest for his sublime ministry, but what he assimilates by reflection and prayer. "If I had to make my theology over again," said Venerable[9] Claude de la Colombière, S. J., "I would give two hours to meditation for every hour of study. It is only by meditation we let truth sink into our mind, and

---

[9] Editor's Note: Now Saint

become able to appreciate and use arguments that are really strong."

Confrater Gabriel was well prepared by his college course at Spoleto to commence the studies proper to our congregation. This curriculum embraces literature, natural and exact science, profane and sacred history, and principally the study of philosophy and theology with canon law, the Holy Scriptures and sacred eloquence. Our young hero completed his philosophical course at Pievetorina with great profit, as F. Germanus his biographer asserts, but he turned far more naturally to the study of the sacred sciences at Isola. Herein he could fully satisfy his ardent desire to know God more intimately that he might love Him more ardently. His progress was as rapid as it was solid, a natural consequence of conscientious application joined to acknowledged talent, and a retentive memory. In our Gabriel there was no fear that the spirit of perfection would grow cold, for he assimilated his fund of knowledge in an atmosphere of prayer, recollection and union with God, zeal for the regular observance, and the practice of interior as well as exterior mortification.

9 The Struggle for Perfection

The most important obligation that a religious contracts toward God by his profession, is that of tending toward perfection; hence the rule prescribes that before a novice is admitted to take the vows he shall be tried by strict inquiry whether he has a fixed purpose of using his utmost efforts to acquire Christian perfection according to our rule and constitutions. This purpose then, has been made the condition of his profession, and it remains the duty of his whole after-life. Confrater Gabriel fully realized this obligation, and more than ever he resolved to become a saint, ever manifesting in deed that this was the continual occupation of his mind, as it was the most ardent desire of his heart.

It must be clear, however, from all that has been said, during the few years he spent in the cloister, that our Gabriel had no opportunity to achieve anything externally grand or noteworthy: the tenor of his life flowed on in the groove of the common observance, and the extreme care with which he sought to hide the perfection of his holiness, makes it all the more difficult to point out anything in his conduct particularly worthy of general admiration. Were a young man living in the secular world to practice all that a religious does, he would be the wonder of his friends, and be held up as an example of extraordinary virtue; but not so in a community where all this is but the common standard. We must needs bear this in mind if we wish to form a correct estimate of Gabriel's perfection;

whilst at the same time, we must understand the nature of spiritual perfection itself. Now, nothing is more carefully impressed upon the young religious, than that perfection does not essentially consist in any external observance, but rather in the union of the soul with God by means of His holy love. On this *interior life* of love, he is taught to concentrate his attention and efforts,—all else is but a means. It is neither the work of one day nor the result of a single effort; it is the occupation and business of a whole life, and is preeminently the work of the *religious* life. Father Norbert, the spiritual director of the servant of God thus testifies to Gabriel's progressive growth in holiness. "I was charged with his direction up to the day of his death, and can, and do testify that he never relented in his spiritual progress whether on account of aridity, weariness or temptation; whether he had the consolation of sensible devotion or not. He ever acted with energy of soul, greatness and generosity of mind, never neglecting himself advertently in anything, ever growing in the perfection of his interior dispositions." "From the beginning of his religious life he set himself to practice with all his strength, the principle inculcated before all others in the novitiate, namely, of walking attentively in the presence of God. By this means, he gradually acquired such interior recollection, and such a state of spiritual disengagement, that nothing whatever, not even work or recreation, could ever distract him in the superior part of his soul. Without difficulty he adverted to every movement of his heart, every grace bestowed on him, every word that God spoke to his soul, or encouragement given his will, every sting of remorse, and every movement of his interior passions. The same diligence with which he performed all his exterior works, he also exercised in his interior acts, repressing and mortifying defective sentiments and interior movements, in order to correspond with God's grace and inspirations; and in all this he was exceedingly faithful. He grieved over his imperfections, he humbled himself deeply on their account before God, he encouraged himself, and resolved to do better in the future, gradually acquiring herein such a degree of virtue, that I could not have desired more. He accomplished all this with a strong will, with generosity and constancy, with alacrity of spirit, and as he used to say himself: *'corde magno et animo volenti'*; with a great heart and a willing mind: avoiding anxiety and fretting on the one hand, as well as indolence on the other. He most carefully guarded himself against useless, and even indifferent thoughts and conversations: he was always engaged with something appertaining either to his office, his studies, or things spiritual. So then what is extraordinary in Confrater Gabriel's life is this: that whatever he did was done with interior dispositions that were altogether extraordinary: with an attention to, and a practice of, the interior life quite uncommon in its degree. This explains the high esteem in which he was held by those that knew him, and accounts for the mature sanctity attained to, by such a young servant of God."

Yet, F. Norbert assures us in another part of his testimony, Confrater Gabriel never showed any singularity in his exterior conduct; in fact, he was decidedly opposed to anything of the kind: but the punctuality, diligence and goodness of his life could not escape the notice of his brethren, who were in consequence greatly edified. These assertions are borne out by the testimony of Gabriel's companions. "What was noticed in him as extraordinary," says F. Bernard, "was that from the day he put on the sacred livery of the Passion, he went on constantly advancing from virtue to virtue with giant steps, in such a manner, that he soon surpassed all his companions in fervor of spirit, tending toward perfection." And F. Xavier deposed: "I was never able to notice in him any willful defect or imperfection, although I was the one out of all his classmates who had the most confidential relations with him."

And this, dear reader, is the testimony resulting from an intimate companionship of six years, by night and by day, in sickness and in health, from the day our Gabriel entered the novitiate, until that of his death! This is the testimony given under oath by priests whose judgment had been ripened by long experience, and who themselves, became so remarkable for their virtue, that they were successively elected to the highest offices of the congregation.

"Many a time," says his director, "have I attentively considered this young man's life, and in my own littleness have I asked myself, whether there was a single virtue belonging to his state, which did not shine forth in him, and whether it would have been possible to wish for anything more excellent in his practice of those virtues; and I have been invariably obliged to answer in the negative. I afterward discovered that several of his fellow-students had asked themselves the same question, and reached the very same conclusion as myself. Such was his 'hunger and thirst for all virtues,' such the assiduity with which he labored for their acquisition, that he never lost an opportunity of practicing them; rather, he purposely sought such opportunities, and knew how to find them everywhere, even in things the most indifferent. Of a truth, it might be said that he lived on virtue, and existed for the sole purpose of practicing it. So evident was his growth in holiness, that it was visible from day to day; but during the last year of his life, such was the abundance of graces imparted to him by his God, and such his correspondence, that he was to me an object of wonder and admiration. His virtue, while ever remaining spontaneous and unaffected was enhanced during that last year by a something of greater majesty and mastery impossible to describe, which awoke in me a sense of deep veneration."

Before proceeding to consider in detail the virtues of this venerable servant of God, it will be well to prefix a few remarks on the nature and practice of virtue in general.

Virtue is a habit or disposition of the soul which inclines us to do good and avoid evil. It is not a mere *negative* disposition; for the absence of a vice does not imply the presence of the contrary virtue; it is a *positive* disposition of the soul inclining to positive acts by which we do the good and avoid the evil. Again, virtue must be *habitual*, for the disposition of the soul must ever be to practice virtuous acts promptly and easily, despite the revolt of our passions. We must also remember that there are two general classes of virtue; one directly infused into the soul by God, the other acquired by repeated acts of our own will, with the concurrence of actual grace.

The infused virtues are called *theological* because they have God for their direct object; the acquired virtues are called moral, inasmuch as they regulate our moral conduct. With the help of God's grace we can grow continually and indefinitely in the theological and moral virtues until the last moment of life. Now, only those who have distinguished themselves by practicing both classes of virtue *in a heroic degree*, are candidates for the sublime honors of canonization, for a saint is before and above all else, a hero of Christian virtue. This heroism is explained to mean a certain eminence and supreme degree of holiness to which man rises by God's grace, above the ordinary strength of others; in short, heroic virtue may be thus defined: A habitual disposition of the soul inclining us heroically to do good, and resist evil. Finally, in the official document of information laid before the Roman commission, we read as follows: "That Confrater Gabriel practiced all manner of virtues in a heroic degree, is clear from the unanimous testimony of all the witnesses, so that he could be held up as an excellent model of the highest perfection. All admired his promptitude and ease in the practice of virtue, and spoke of him as a saint. It was evident that he kept before his eyes and in his heart the examples of Christ and His saints, whom he ever strove to imitate with the greatest earnestness. He was ever advancing in holiness, no matter what the hindrance might be; like a valiant soldier (whose courage is tried on the field of battle) the harder the struggle, the more brightly did his perfection shine forth, so that all his acts of virtue might truly be called heroic. In this holy exercise he persevered until death, and no one was ever found to contest his claim to exalted virtue."

This opinion has been shared by illustrious men,—cardinals, bishops, generals of religious orders—who having examined into his life, petitioned the Holy See for his beatification and canonization.

10 Temperance and Mortification

The word *temperance* is popularly identified with abstinence from intoxicating drinks, or at least with moderation in the use made of them. Now, although the habit of sobriety belongs to the cardinal virtue of temperance, it is only one of its practical applications. The proper office of this virtue is to keep a due restraint on all the passions of our animal nature. For him that seeks to follow Christ, the first step is to conquer self. "If any man wishes to come after Me, let him deny himself." Such a one must resist the unruly affections of his heart, his love for the world and the things that are in it, the concupiscences of the eyes and the flesh, and the pride of life. Now this is precisely the scope and the aim of the virtue of temperance.

Though excess in eating and drinking be the least difficult of all our passions to overcome, self-control in these particulars is an indispensable condition for one who wishes to lead a *spiritual* life. St. Vincent de Paul used to say that mortification of the appetite was the ABC of perfection. "At table, let the brethren conduct themselves with sobriety and temperance," says our holy rule, "for the more freely one indulges his appetites, the more closely and painfully will he be tormented." "If thou give to thy soul her desires, she will make thee a joy to thy enemies." (Ecclesiasticus 18:31)

From the very beginning of his religious career, therefore, Gabriel set his face against this vice; and among his resolutions we read: "I will never exceed in quantity. I will not eat with avidity, but rather with reserve and modesty, subjecting my appetite to reason." How faithful he was to this self-imposed rule, his director tells us: "The greatest difficulty I met with in regulating his exterior mortification, was to give him a fixed rule that would free him from all uncertainty in the matter of food and drink. But God enabled me to guide him so that his health might not be impaired, that he might have the strength needed for the exercises of the religious observance, and the due prosecution of his studies. At first he was somewhat concerned from fear of excess, but gradually he freed himself from anxiety by the practice of obedience, and succeeded in maintaining that measure of temperance which avoids all extremes equally." Again we read in his resolutions: "I will not speak of what relates to food, and much less will I complain. I will not take food outside of the appointed time. I will be satisfied with what is set before me, without complaining either in word or thought, mindful that I have vowed poverty, and that our Lord permits some things to test the sincerity of my promise." One of his companions having grumbled about the scantiness of his supper, Gabriel chided him gently, saying: "What's the use of complaining? I'm sure we had enough, after all." If what he ate was not to his liking, Gabriel took occasion to practice a little mortification, remembering that our Divine Savior not only sometimes had no bread to break His fast, but during His agony on the cross, He had not even a drop of water to quench His thirst. If his food pleased him, he diverted his attention by listening more closely to the reading, or by making pious reflections of his own. If he felt particularly inclined to gratify his appetite, he would mortify himself by waiting a little, and eating more slowly, thus seasoning everything with mortification, and sanctifying a merely animal occupation. He that *seeks* pleasure in the gratification of the senses, will never *find* pleasure in spiritual things.

Temperance is guarded and perfected by the practice of mortification, and without the habitual exercise of self-restraint even in things lawful, no one can advance in spirituality. These "fruits of penance" may scandalize a sensual world, but they are dear to all who would follow in the footsteps of a scourged and crucified Master. "I chastise my body," says the apostle, "and bring it into subjection." "Gabriel's love of self-denial was well shown," so reads the summary of the Process,"by the selection he made of the rigid institute in which he chose to spend his life. Yet how much more rigid would he not have made its rule," the same document continues, "had not his superiors moderated his ardent desire to add every kind of mortification thereunto." It appears that the Master of Novices had been somewhat condescending in this respect, so that F. Norbert, after undertaking Gabriel's direction, met with some difficulty in keeping his fervent disciple within proper limits. "I constantly found in him," this Father writes, "a great spirit of both interior and exterior mortification, as well as a habitual desire of practicing it. In regard to exterior mortification, he had such a strong inclination for corporal austerities, that had I not watched over him and restrained him, his fervor would have prompted him to perform so many, and of such a nature, that in a short time he would have ruined his constitution. In fact, I found him immoderately inclined to such things in the beginning, and hard to be convinced on this special point. In order to obtain permission for certain mortifications which I deemed inappropriate, he would urge upon me all the reasons he could imagine, and that with such cleverness that frequently he would have gained his point had I not been extremely careful. When I spoke to him of his delicate constitution, 'Why,' he would answer, 'if we are to pay attention to such things we'll never do anything at all;' or, again: 'All that is nothing for such a sinner as myself.' Many saints though poor in health and constitution, practiced far more. It was said of St. Aloysius that on his deathbed he would feel remorse for the rigorous penances he performed, yet he was not troubled at all;" and then he would often add, "I guess the saints were singular on this score."

But as Gabriel advanced in virtue, he gradually corrected this immoderate inclination, becoming at last very docile to the least intimation of his director, saying: "In being obedient in this matter, there is a double gain: first on account of the mortification itself, and then by reason of the self-denial enjoined by obedience." For a long time (to cite a single instance) he sought permission to wear a chain set with sharp points. Though always refused, he would still beg for it with modest persistence. His director replied: "You want to wear the little chain! I tell you that what you really stand in need of is a chain on your will; yes, that's what you need!—Go away, don't speak to me about it. And he retired deeply mortified. Another time he was asking leave for the same thing: 'well, yes!' I said, 'wear it by all means; but you must wear it outside your habit, and in public, too, that all may see what a man of great mortification you are!' Though stung to the quick, he did as I told him, and wore it as I directed; besides, to satisfy his thirst for penances by giving him more than he asked, I made fun of him before his companions; but he, without ever replying, without showing the slightest impatience, took everything in silence, nor would he even ask to be dispensed from thus becoming the laughing-stock of all."

Unable to satisfy his craving for external penances, because prevented by obedience, Gabriel found means to mortify himself interiorly in everything. Whether eating or drinking, standing or kneeling, during recreation or repose, he found ways to contradict nature and self-love: yet, he acted with such dexterity and naturalness that no one could perceive it, unless he were acquainted with the secrets of his soul. His eyes, ears, taste and feeling had each their own mortification. He was particularly zealous in such practices during the triduums and novenas which preceded the great festivals. At such times, his preparations consisted not in the mere recital of a few extra prayers, but in a renewed application to overcome himself interiorly in everything. Before and after Holy Communion, as a remote preparation, and continued thanksgiving, he likewise redoubled his acts of self-denial. He encouraged himself in these practices by meditating on the sufferings of Jesus, the dolors[10] of his compassionate Mother, and the great truths of faith, thus maintaining the fervor of his penitential spirit undiminished until the day of his death. The following maxims we find written in Gabriel's book of resolutions: "I will profit by every occasion of mortification that occurs, without seeking after them." "I will fulfill exactly my ordinary duties, mortifying self in whatever would prove an obstacle to perfect obedience." "I will mortify my eyes and my tongue; I will not leave my cell without necessity; I will not inquire after anything through curiosity; I will check my desire to talk; and I will increase the number of such like acts every day." And again: "I will mortify myself in ordinary things, and in whatever I feel inclined to do, saying in my heart: O my God ! I will not do this thing through mere inclination, but because it is Thy will."

To all these generous resolutions we will add but one more; but though exceedingly brief in words, it is the most comprehensive and most heroic of all: "I will strive to resist all my inclinations."

However great the care Gabriel took to conceal these acts of virtue from all except his director, they could not escape the notice of the most observant and experienced among his companions. One of them, F. Bernard[11] (afterward general of the whole congregation) testifies as follows: "Considering the

---

[10] Editor's Note: Dolor means pain, grief, or sorrow in Latin. The author is referring here to the 7 Sorrows of Our Lady.

[11] Editor's Note: Father Bernardo Maria of Jesus was beatified on October 16, 1988.

circumstances of Confrater Gabriel's life as a secular, to behold him now in religion, and even from the very beginning, so detached from all things, so humble, obedient, reserved and delicate of conscience, must necessarily impress one with the conviction that he set about the reformation of himself with a more than ordinary spirit of mortification:— all those who treated with him in daily and familiar converse could not help but recognize this fact. He did not practice any extraordinary external penances; but this was not for lack of desire, but solely because such penances were prohibited by obedience, to which he submitted with the docility of a child. The fervent youth, however, knew well how to compensate for this loss; for beside the exact observance of his rule, he was most attentive at every moment, and in every action, even the most indifferent, not only to sanctify the same by the most exalted intentions, but also to accompany them all with some self-imposed penance."

11 Chastity

For a beginner there is no virtue that requires a greater struggle for its mastery, there is no virtue that gives a greater victory over self, than chastity: likewise, there is no virtue that makes a boy more manly, and therefore more noble. The reason of this is to be found in the fact that in the ardent years of youth, chastity can be acquired and maintained only by unceasing combat; and even as the soldier becomes valiant by having to face danger, so the good Christian youth cannot but perfect his manliness by courageously resisting sensual temptation. Habitual concessions to one's grosser passions lower the soul to a slavery, the ignominy of which is soon stamped on the very looks and whole demeanor of a profligate youth; whereas chastity impresses upon the countenance a spiritual and manly beauty, to which even the infidel and the scoffer are forced to pay homage.

Now, this most beautiful virtue which maketh earthly men like unto the angels of heaven, shone in a remarkable manner in Confrater Gabriel. Thanks to a special protection of the Immaculate Virgin, he preserved unsullied the white garment of baptismal innocence amidst all the dangers of the world, but it was only in the sanctuary of the cloister, that this virtue was made perfect. "I find it impossible to express in words," writes his director, "the love that Confrater Gabriel nourished for the angelic virtue, the jealousy with which he watched over it, and the care he took to avoid all that might in the least tarnish its lustre. It would be necessary to have seen him and known him, to form an adequate idea of his virginal modesty." It may be said that from the time of his entrance into the religious state, he truly emulated the angelic St. Aloysius, to whom indeed, he has been compared by such eminent judges as Cardinals Parocchi, Richard, Goossens, Canossa, Manara, di Pietro, La Valetta, Vaughan, de Ruggiero, and others; but above all by our Holy Father, Leo XIII.

It should be remembered that chastity is an acquired virtue, and that the effort required on Gabriel's part was proportioned to his ardent and affectionate temper. He was not then a stranger to the harassing temptations of youth; his chastity was rather a glorious victory over the common foe. "He was so diligent in driving away every thought and temptation against decency," relates F. Norbert, "that during the whole time that I directed him, I do not remember that even once he had any doubt or fear of having failed in any manner whatsoever." But then, he used such circumspection in avoiding danger, that when reading or studying, if he fell upon anything suggestive of evil, he passed it over at once, however interesting it might appear. He even said that he would never read the "History of Heresies," written by St. Alphonsus, because their origin and progress are always bound up with the spirit of impurity, sometimes indeed scandalously and grossly so. Those familiar with the biographies of the reformation worthies will agree that he was not much mistaken.[12]

It is not uncommon even with conscientious young people in the world, to gratify their curiosity as long as it does not prove to be directly sinful; they take it to be their privilege to see and hear and enjoy everything that is not positively bad. That Gabriel, as a secular, labored under the same dangerous error, we have already seen from his fondness for theatres and balls, novels and other worldly vanities. But from the time of his conversion he fully understood that the concupiscence of the eyes must necessarily lead to the concupiscence of the flesh; and that the freedom of the children of the world is incompatible with the purity of the children of God.

Hence to preserve intact the angelic virtue, he began to practice the mortification of his senses, and this to such a degree, that soon he became an object of admiration even to the most fervent; everything seeming to him as if it did not exist, so completely did he stifle all his natural inclinations. One of the first habits to which novices are accustomed is custody of their eyes. "Let the brethren," says the rule, "keep a diligent guard over their senses, but especially restrain their eyes." The moral axiom that "unrestrained freedom in gazing about is incompatible with purity of heart," was known even to the pagans of old. Hence our Gabriel from his very first days in

---

[12] Editor's Note: St. Alphonsus Liguori was declared a doctor of the Church not long after St. Gabriel's death. His unwillingness to read such a work, even though a most holy soul wrote it, is a remarkable sign of St. Gabriel's devotion to purity of spirit.

the novitiate, before he received the religious habit, made a covenant with his eyes which he scrupulously observed to his death. If perchance he met a person of the other sex, he would either turn his eyes in some other direction, or else fix them upon the little crucifix or the image of Our Lady of Dolors, which we have on our beads. But he did this with such a total absence of constraint or affectation that he seemed to act as naturally in this as in all else. This reserve was particularly striking when on rare occasions the students happened to enter the house of some benefactor. No doubt such circumspection will appear exaggerated to those of a worldly spirit; yet this was the common practice of the saints of God:—either then, *their* austerity or *our* carelessness must surely be at fault.

With the avenues of his senses so jealously guarded, it became easy for him to control his imagination. Nor was he satisfied with this: knowing that our mind is ever active, he took care to be always provided with holy thoughts, promptly banishing whatever was merely indifferent or simply useless. With all watchfulness he kept his heart since life issues forth from it. He guarded himself from any affection that was not evidently holy, and herein he was truly singular. He thus wrote in his book of resolutions: "I will be reserved toward those to whom I feel most inclined, prudently avoiding their presence and conversation." His whole conduct was a reflection of the rule left by St. Paul of the Cross[13] to his sons: "Let

---

[13] Editor's Note: the founder of the Passionists.

the brethren be humble, let them resist their passions, mortify the flesh, apply diligently to prayer, in all things act with circumspection, attribute nothing to their own strength, place all their confidence in God, and work out their salvation with fear and trembling. Let them entertain a pious and ardent devotion toward the Immaculate Virgin Mother of God, strive to imitate her sublime virtues, and to merit her seasonable protection amid so many dangers."

Our Gabriel was habitually so modest in his exterior that he did not even know the religious with whom he lived, save by their voice or gait; and on the other hand, none of his companions could tell with certainty the color of his eyes. He always walked in a most modest manner with downcast eyes, according to the advice of St. Benedict, St. Ignatius, as well as our holy Founder, but in all this his demeanor was so natural that it did not obtrude itself upon the notice of others as a singularity, whilst his very presence breathed forth the angelical purity of his soul. The mere sight of him moved all to piety and devotion; and it often happened that when persons met him out walking in the midst of his companions, they were seen to stop on the road and gaze upon him with compunction, and then follow him with their eyes after he had passed on. Seminarians who came to the retreat to make the spiritual exercises before their ordination, could hardly keep their eyes off him whenever he chanced to come near them; "and," continues his director, "I could notice that Confrater Gabriel's modesty had a singular influence in moving them to fervor. Quite a number of them would not leave till I had allowed them the privilege of a conversation with him. They left his presence filled with fervor and compunction, and for a long time they retained the salutary impression made upon them."

This singular reserve and delicacy of the servant of God is not to be confounded with morbid prudery, a thing utterly estranged from virtue. Gabriel's sensitiveness was rather a divine instinct which made him feel no longer at home in flesh and blood, as long as they were subject to original corruption. "Unhappy man that I am," cried out the apostle, "who will deliver me from the body of this death?" "His spirit indeed groaneth being burdened, until his earthly house of habitation should be dissolved." (2 Corinthians 5) Abstracting, however, from extraordinary grace, let us remember that in certain phases of exterior modesty the saints are sometimes less to be imitated than admired. Their extreme delicacy must be attributed to a state, of which the sensual world has no clear idea, and utterly no sympathy. In grosser beings the flesh seems to become too heavy for the spirit, and weighs it down to the earth and its pleasure; but in more refined natures, the spirit seems to emancipate itself, and lift the body up to regions not yet quite congenial to its present condition, until "that which is mortal shall be swallowed up by life."

12 His Humility

To conquer the pride of life requires no less of a struggle than to overcome the concupiscence of the flesh, and it would be difficult to say which of these two is the greater obstacle to a spiritual life; were it not that experience, as well as the masters of asceticism, teach that pride is impurity's parent. "God resisteth the proud and giveth His grace to the humble." True humility is the safeguard, as well as the foundation of all the other virtues. Hence, there is no virtue in which the young religious is more thoroughly grounded than this from the very beginning, and hence, too, our Gabriel, with the instinct of divine grace, strove to lay the solid foundations of sanctity in the depths of the profoundest humility. He was so penetrated with its importance, that frequently in conversation he would bring up some appropriate sentence from Scripture, or a maxim of the saints, and particularly this one of our Holy Founder, that "one grain of pride will cause a mountain of sanctity to crumble."

But Confrater Gabriel was a doer to the word, and not a hearer only, as his companions attest: what he preached, he first practiced. In his book of resolutions we read as follows: "I will not utter a word that might in the least turn to my praise." And again: "I will not take pleasure in any praise bestowed upon me; on the contrary, I will despise it, as bestowed upon one who does not deserve it." ..."I will never excuse myself when I am corrected or blamed, nor even resent anything interiorly; much less throw the blame upon others." ..."I will never

speak of the faults of others, even though public; nor will I ever show want of esteem for them whether in their presence or behind their back. I will speak of all with praise and esteem."
..."I will not judge ill of anyone; I will, on the contrary, show the good opinion I have of them by covering up their faults."
..."I will consider everyone as my superior, not merely in theory, but in practice, treating all with humility and reverence."
..."I will avail myself with patience and alacrity of every opportunity of humiliation that presents itself." ..."Every morning and evening I will practice some acts of humility, and endeavor gradually to increase their number." ...The last two resolutions clearly show that in this matter Gabriel was aiming at perfection by the only efficacious way known, namely a vigorous and constant *exercise* of virtue: for just as science is not acquired without study, nor patience without suffering, so neither can humility be made perfect without humiliations. In the religious life there are various practices conducive to this end. Taken from the canonical penances of old, they are debasing to man's pride, but they enable those who perform them in the proper spirit, to follow manfully in the footsteps of a Divine Master who humbled Himself even unto the death of the Cross. Penetrated with such sentiments our Gabriel composed the following prayer, the solidity of whose doctrine is rivaled by its unction:

"Behold me at Thy feet, O Lord, begging for pity and for mercy! What wilt Thou lose in granting me a great love for Thee, a profound humility, great purity of heart, mind and body; fraternal charity, intense sorrow for having offended

Thee, and the grace to offend Thee no more?—What wilt Thou lose, O my God, by enabling me to receive worthily Thy Son in Holy Communion?—in assisting me to act through love of Thee in all my thoughts, works, penances and prayers?—by granting me the grace of loving Thy holy Mother most tenderly and trustfully; the grace of final perseverance in my vocation, and of dying a good and holy death?

"I am a beggar asking for alms, covered with sores and rags. O see my misery! Here is my proud head, my cold heart, yes, my stony heart. Here is my mind filled with worldly thoughts, my will inclined only to evil, my body rebellious to every good work.

"Help me, O my God!...do help me to correct myself. This grace I ask through Thine own goodness, through Thine infinite mercy. To obtain it, I offer Thee the merits of Jesus Christ, our Saviour and Lord. I have no merits of my own, I am destitute; but, His wounds will be my plea; *Vulnera tua merita mea*. Had I shed my blood for love of Thee, like Thy Son, wouldst Thou not grant me this favor? How much more oughtest Thou to hear me now, since He shed *His* for me?

"Art Thou not He who hast promised in Thy Gospel that whatsoever I ask for the good of my soul Thou wilt grant: 'Ask and you shall receive...?' Now, as Thou canst not withdraw Thy word, I beseech Thee to hear me. I beseech Thee through Thine infinite goodness; through the heart of Thy Son wounded with love for me; through the infinite charity of Thy eternal Spirit; through the love Thou bearest Thy most holy daughter Mary; and for the honor of the whole heavenly court, into which I ask Thee one day to admit me. Amen."

This prayer was written by the servant of God, shortly after his entrance into the cloister: it was the first flower of his fervor and exhales the fragrance of rare virtue. From his written resolutions then, we can easily see Gabriel's ideas concerning the excellence of humility; let us now hear from those who knew him best, how he put those ideas into practice.

Speaking of his holy disciple, F. Norbert deposes in the processes: "In the exercise and pursuit of holy humility, he followed the same method he had adopted in acquiring all the other virtues; that is, he directed his attention principally to his interior, stripping his heart of its vices, and clothing it with the opposite virtues. He kept before his eyes his own nothingness and misery; his former life in the world, his propensity to evil, his unfaithfulness to God, his weakness and helplessness. With all these motives he was intimately penetrated, especially during the time of meditation; and by this means he attained such a humble opinion of himself that he greatly feared and distrusted self, relying in all things solely on the assistance of God's holy grace. He often said: 'Of myself I can do nothing....Of myself I am capable only of sin, yes, even of the greatest crimes.' He spoke thus because he was intimately convinced of these truths in his heart: and I remember well that in all he did, he placed no reliance on his own powers, or efforts, or talents, even in matters of no great importance. However, this mean opinion of himself and his worth made him neither melancholy, nor slothful; on the contrary it filled him with courage to undertake whatever was pleasing to God, because he always maintained a strong and filial confidence in his heart toward the Almighty. And truly, his confidence was not misplaced, for in whatever he undertook the Lord blessed him with success. Never, as far as I can remember, did a single word escape from his lips that might even indirectly have turned to his praise; never did he refer to anything that would redound to his glory, whether with relation to his secular or his religious career; whatever was known of him in this respect came not from him, but from others, since he studiously abstained from giving his brethren any information that might have increased their regard for him. His extreme modesty edified me greatly."

F. Francis Xavier, the most critical of all his companions says of him: "Never was Confrater Gabriel known to refer to anything that might in the least turn to his glory; of his distinguished relations in secular life he never spoke."

"He shunned as the very pest," F. Norbert continues, "any shadow of complacency and vainglory about anything he had ever done or was doing; being very cautious lest he might be deceived by self-love. For instance: Having one day made for himself one of those *Signs* or badges of the Passion worn by us on our habit and cloak, it turned out to be a beautiful piece of work; but Gabriel insisted that I should let him exchange it for the Sign of another religious, lest his own should occasion some thought of vainglory, and I had to yield. Many of his companions, too, have left their written testimony that they never heard from him any expression of self-praise. He took delight

His Humility

in wearing clothes that had been used by others, or anything that was poor or ill-fitting. Everything in him was adorned with modesty and humility. His constant self-abasement in word and deed was itself so hidden, so natural and spontaneous, that it did not bear the appearance of humiliation. He was an enemy to affectation and exaggeration in anything, but above all in matters of humility and humiliation. Nor was he less averse to anything like effusiveness in self-abasement; he carefully concealed his very sentiments of humility, speaking as he felt with naturalness and simplicity, giving the matter no further thought."

"Whenever he was subjected to some humiliation or was derided, whether on set purpose or merely as a trial to his virtue, he would assimilate it interiorly and relish his abjection to such a degree of contentment, that it would be hard to describe it properly."

"It was his custom neither to excuse nor to defend himself, but simply to suffer and be silent; and if occasionally by mistake he was judged guilty of something that he did not do, he could hardly contain his satisfaction and joy. He looked upon all others as his superiors and considered himself everybody's servant. When saying 'culpa' in the refectory or in chapter,[14] when performing the usual penances or humbling himself before anyone, it was easily seen that he really meant what he

---

[14] By "culpa" we mean the public acknowledgment of one's exterior faults against the rules. The "chapter" is a convention of the religious community. It is called *general*, if composed of representatives of the whole order: *provincial* if of the province, *local* if of the individual community.

was saying or doing. Often have I noticed how dexterously he sought to be the least of all, to take the lowest place, to be served last, and to choose the worst of everything. All this, however, he did so cleverly and so naturally, that unless one were used to his ways, and acquainted with his interior, he would never have suspected but that these things had so happened of themselves, yet they left everyone unconsciously edified. Many a time have I noticed that when some particular attention was paid him, he felt so great a repugnance that he showed it externally; and on the other hand, he would often ask me to reprehend and humble him in public, and when I neglected to do so for want of reason, or because I could find no fitting occasion, he would come to me and gently complain. When I did happen to correct him, he would at once kneel down and remain in that posture until I told him to arise. If I left the room without telling him to stand up, he would humbly remain in that position even for a considerable time, either till I returned, or sent a fellow-student with the needed permission. I often reprimanded him for what I knew he did not do. At such times he never excused himself either to me or to his companions, either then or afterward: neither by word, look nor gesture did he show that he was not guilty of what he was being blamed for. Even when I did not mean to reprimand but merely to warn him of something, he would immediately kneel down with a respect and humility that faithfully bespoke his interior dispositions. The reprehension over, he would say on resuming his seat, 'Well, I must correct myself....I richly deserved it....' Withal, his confidence in me was not in any way lessened, but rather increased."

It was often noticed that he gladly occupied himself in the meanest domestic employments, "for in these," he used to say, "we gain more glory, than by doing other things." Of course, both the devil and his own passions fought hard against him, seeking to thwart him in these virtuous pursuits, but temptation would only make him the humbler, and would seem to encourage him the more, to acquire the very perfection of humility and to exercise it.

"He was most faithful in manifesting to me the secrets of his heart; and the greater the difficulty he felt, the more valiantly would he conquer self. At times, too, when there was no necessity of conferring with me, he would nevertheless come for the sole reason of overcoming the repugnance and difficulty he experienced, in all his temptations against humility, I do not remember that he ever once listened to the sentiments suggested by the devil or his own passions. He had also this practice: when he perceived anything in himself, which if known to others would bring him humiliation and contempt, he would find means to call public attention to it: but if circumstances rendered this inadvisable through motives of prudence, he would make it known to me alone." On all such occasions he never lost his equanimity of soul, nor was he unduly irritated against himself: he simply and peacefully entered thereby into a fuller knowledge of all his weakness, and a deeper contempt of himself.

13 His Meekness

After he has won the victory over the concupiscence of the eyes, and the concupiscence of the flesh, there remains to the soldier of Jesus Christ one more enemy to conquer, namely the pride of life. Now this vice is manifested in a twofold way: by vainglory in his understanding, and anger in his will; it must therefore be conquered by the virtues of humility and meekness.

Man by pride aspired to be equal to God; God by the Incarnation lowered Himself to the level of man, and then said: "Learn of Me, because I am meek and humble of heart, and you shall find rest to your souls." (Matthew 11:29) "From the time I undertook the spiritual direction of Confrater Gabriel," says F. Norbert, "I examined the practices of mortification which he was wont to perform. I suppressed whatever seemed excessive, considering his constitution, as well as the austerities of the Passionist observance; but at the same time, I gave him wide scope for such mortifications as could not overtax his bodily strength, and above all for the exercise of *interior* virtue. The latter I insisted on as the most important, and thereunto he applied himself with all the energy of his soul."

This self-conquest naturally showed itself externally. "No man who had lived with him as a secular, and had become the daily witness of his religious life," says F. Bernard, "would have taken him for the same person: all his vanity, levity, impatience, arrogance—in fine all those habits that were so noticeable in him before, vanished on his entrance into religion, and there remained of his former personality only those beautiful traits which afterward blossomed into perfect virtue." F. Xavier, another of his fellow-students, speaks of Gabriel in the same strain, and then adds: "Never did he utter a word that might hurt anyone's feelings; never did he show that he had been wounded in his own. I well remember that frequently I took pleasure in trying his patience, but his only retort was a quiet smile." Yet the reader will recollect that from his very infancy our hero's predominant passion was that of anger, and how frequently in spite of his good resolutions he had to deplore many a sudden outburst of almost ungovernable feeling. In the cloister his victory was complete: passion would no sooner arise, but it was conquered by a resolute will; then would he humble himself deeply for having had even that first spontaneous motion of anger, and thus in spite of his sensitive temper, he became for all a model of patience and meekness, growing steadily in every degree of self-conquest as his life went on. His meekness thus was an *acquired* virtue, the fruit of an unceasing warfare that required the exercise of heroic virtue. Yet several of his companions who had lived with him for years, never noticed a sign of the internal struggle he had to undergo to conquer self; they afterward declared that they always thought that Gabriel's facility in practicing self-control was merely the effect of his "good nature"! "It was by continual recollection," as F. Norbert says, "that he contrived to keep a strict guard over his heart, and over self-love in particular. By the light that God gave him, he detected the uprising of every passion, (and this with a degree of clearness quite unusual even in interior souls): and was extremely prompt in repressing and contradicting them."

In his book of resolutions we read: "I will shut my heart against disquiet of any kind: against sadness and displeasure, and much more against anything like aversion or revenge. I will cultivate peace of heart, and therefore I will not give any sign of impatience either in word or action. I will suppress at once all sudden movements, and all affections that might ever so slightly cloud my mind." And knowing in the light of God, that envy of others and an overestimate of our own excellence are the causes of our anger, he lays the axe at the root of the evil when he writes in another of his resolutions: "I will rejoice in the good done by others, and will account it a fault to feel any sentiment of envy; neither will I allow myself to be interested in vain things."

14 His Cheerfulness

When a Christian by means of temperance has overcome his evil passions, he may then reasonably turn to the more consoling work of developing all that good that is latent in him, by the cardinal virtue of justice. Now justice may be explained as being the rectitude of intention which seeks to know the right in order to do it. It is sometimes called "the sense of duty": prompting us to give to God the things that are God's and to all men their due.

Considering the many limitations of our double nature, we were evidently intended to live in society, therefore "hath God given every man commandment concerning his brother." Created in the image of a God of infinite goodness, we are so to act that we may ever prove ourselves to be worthy children of our heavenly Father "who maketh His sun to rise upon the good and bad, and raineth upon the just and the unjust." (Matthew 5:45) And what is that sunshine that we are to shed upon our neighbors, what the refreshing dew, but that spiritual cheerfulness of which the apostle wrote, saying: "Rejoice in the Lord always; again I say, rejoice?" (Philippians 4:4)

Nature had given our Gabriel an abiding cheerfulness of character, but divine grace perfected and transfigured it. "While still a secular," writes Bonaccia, "serenity ever shone on his brow: his glance, his smile, the accent of his voice, all revealed a heart in which joy was predominant." In a religious, freed from all worldly cares and fears, we naturally expect to see a peaceful joy, which gilds and renders attractive both the state itself and those that are held to represent it. The children of St. Paul of the Cross are no exception in this respect. From the very beginning, a winning cheerfulness has been their characteristic: it offsets their austerities, and rewards them for their faithfulness. Yet even in their midst, Gabriel's companions could not but wonder, and look with a holy envy at his ever peaceful countenance. For where is the man whose horizon is not sometimes obscured by a passing cloud?—where is human nature to be found so tempered by Christian fortitude and generosity, but that experiences moments of depression? Nothing of the kind, however, was noticed in our hero: not even for a moment did any of his fellow-religious see him under the influence of either weariness or sadness.

It could hardly be that this unalterable serenity of mind was a mere gift of nature which cost him nothing: he too had his temptations, moments of interior depression, when all seems dark and useless, but he never allowed these feelings to overmaster him: his resolute will triumphed over his natural weakness, bearing him on in magnificent reaches toward the heights of manly holiness and religious perfection.

If our Gabriel avoided the extreme of peevishness and sadness, likewise did he guard against the equally perilous extreme of boisterousness, that sure index of an inconstant and superficial character. F. Bernard speaking of his holy companion says: "He was the delight of his brethren. Whoever had to deal with him was struck with wonder at his unruffled disposition, joined as it was to the most amiable manners." "His presence," says his biographer, "was like a ray of heavenly sunshine that fell upon the very soul of those whom he approached: it was as if a source of unearthly sweetness welled up from his heart and flowed out in streams of joy through his eyes and lips and whole demeanor." He was an enemy to all singularity: he had none of that moroseness, that sour and silent spirit of criticism, that chills the mirth of recreation and destroys fraternal charity: his manners were natural but refined, his conversation often tinged with contagious humor; and even the witty pleasantry and innocent joke, which hurts nobody and cheers the heart of man, were by no means foreign to him.

It would be very hard to describe faithfully his habitual mien: it was either a joyful modesty, or a religious joyfulness; for as F. Bernard remarks: "He never separated this cheerful amiability from the most reserved modesty of manner. He was never guilty of word or gesture that savored of levity; rather, everything he did and said was accompanied with a certain reserve, which in turn was adorned with a nameless spiritual unction; so that while his whole conduct was composed and natural, and his conversation charming, both always proved greatly edifying and enticed to virtue. All this became more apparent at a time when naturally it might have been quite the reverse: that is during his last lingering illness. Even then his ingenuous heartiness was like a magnet that drew his brethren to his bed of sickness and kept them most willingly there. It was more than Christian charity and fraternal benevolence that made them anxious to wait on him: the real reason was that the sanctified pleasantness of the invalid himself was like a bright sun, in whose light and heat they daily basked. His body, never very robust, was then attenuated by weakness, his face emaciated by sickness, yet the joyfulness of his soul seemed only to increase, as his bodily strength declined."

Confrater Gabriel was of medium height, his countenance graceful and composed, ever lit up with a winning smile; his eyes were large and deep, intelligent and bright, modestly lowered under well-arched brows; his forehead was high and broad, his hair dark, his face oval and symmetrical. Such is the pen portrait given us by his friend and first biographer, Paul Bonaccia.[15] "His manners were very attractive," says F. Norbert, "his ways naturally refined, his speech was prompt and appropriate, never failing to engage and hold the attention." In a word, he united many beautiful qualities in an uncommon degree, and it was no wonder that he won the esteem and love of all, even aside from the virtue and sanctity with which all this natural perfection was crowned. Whilst his

---

[15] NOTE. *The Portrait of the Blessed Gabriel*—The picture given as the frontispiece of this book is made after a painting by the Italian artist, Professor Grandi, preserved in our retreat of the Scala Santa in Rome. The original painting is so well done, that artists declare it to be impossible to reproduce its expression exactly. There is no authentic portrait of the blessed servant of God in existence: Grandi's having been made from the descriptions of those who knew him best. F. Norbert says: "Oh, how much more handsome was the dear servant of God!" However, *this* has become the popular representation of the holy youth; and strange to say, in the various manifestations in which Gabriel has appeared to those who have invoked him, he has shown himself so strikingly like his picture, that on seeing it, they declared "that the young Passionist looked just like that!"

appearance was attractive, his conversation forbade anything like familiarity; while inspiring confidence, it commanded respect. He was an enemy to every degree of hypocrisy and falsehood, avoided all flattery and artifice, considerate yet candid and truthful. In public or in private he respected the good name and reputation of his neighbor; affectionate to all, bearing with all, and excusing all, he never gave any occasion for complaint. To those who had recently entered the novitiate he showed particular kindness, making them feel that they were surrounded by true brethren in their new home. Whilst he judged himself the least of all the community, he was fearful lest he might be thought more of than others. So sensitive was he upon this point, that at times he fancied he was treated with more consideration than his brethren, and dreaded that anyone should thereby be deprived of what was his due. More will be said on this interesting and practical subject in a later chapter, when we speak of the supernatural charity which inspired and ennobled his cheerfulness and his considerateness.

15 His Spirit of Religion

If justice requires that man fulfill his duties to himself and his neighbors, much more does it demand that he acknowledge and discharge his obligations to God, his Creator and last end. The greatest act of this virtue is sacrifice, by which we offer something of our own, in acknowledgment of God's supreme dominion: and in the case of a member of a religious order, this supreme act is done when he makes his "profession," and pronounces his vows. By these vows a man sacrifices to God all that is his: his body, his possessions, his liberty: he makes of himself a holocaust so complete that there is nothing substantial left. When this religious profession is officially accepted in God's name by the Church, it separates us from the world to consecrate us irrevocably to the Lord: a consecration much more excellent than that of the sacred vessels of the altar, since it is the result of a deliberate and hearty choice. As soon then as a novice has caught the true spirit of his vocation, he looks forward to the day of his profession with an ever-increasing longing. How eagerly our Gabriel yearned for it we have already seen. He always referred to it as "the memorable 25th of September." He thoroughly understood the dignity of the new state of life upon which he had entered, and correspondingly great was his gratitude to God for his vocation, and his resolute purpose to live up to it. The essential difference between the religious and the secular state is the consecration which a religious makes of his whole life to the service of God; therefore, as long as he is guided by his rule, all his acts become acts of the virtue of religion; whereas for seculars, the only possible acts of this virtue are such as refer directly and immediately to the divine worship. With all the fervor of his earnest soul, Gabriel undertook to become a perfect man by living up to the Passionist rule which he accepted on the day of his profession. His director testifies on this point as follows: "Gabriel was truly a model to his companions, and even to his seniors, in his observance of rule." In fact, scarcely had he become a novice, than he showed himself as faithful as though he had spent many years in religion, and found in every act of the common observance, that relish which one finds only in the most congenial occupation. For the holy rule, he entertained the highest regard, considering it as the law by which he would one day be judged. He would read it only with uncovered head, and in taking up or putting down the little book, he would reverently kiss it. "I will keep every rule, even the least," he wrote among his other resolutions, and he was so faithful to this promise, that he could not have kept it better, says one of his companions: while another deposed under oath that he never saw the servant of God breaking any rule, even inadvertently. "He was careful in keeping all the rules without exception," writes F. Norbert, "because he regarded them all *as* rules, and because he had freely bound himself to keep them. Never did he transgress any of them knowingly; nay, great would be his sorrow when sickness or some other unavoidable hindrance rendered some point of the rule impossible; and it was plainly visible how much he was affected by not being able to be with the community. More than once," continues F. Norbert, "having dispensed him on the score of ill-health, he feared, lest I should have been moved by too much considerateness, and he actually had recourse to the higher superiors whenever they chanced to be available: but when they gave him to understand that they approved of my dispensation, he made use of it with all simplicity. In his observance of the rules, he never took into account the discomfort that his fidelity would entail; on the contrary, this was for him an additional reason for regularity, since it offered him the opportunity of practicing several virtues simultaneously. Had his superiors allowed themselves to be influenced by the eagerness which he always displayed, to observe the rule at any cost, he would have insisted on keeping many points, from which moral impossibility would naturally have excused him. Besides, the fact that he was dispensed from any act of the common observance, did not seem to him a sufficient reason to extend the dispensation to other points, though the same reasons existed for both." "When I went to reside in the Retreat of Isola," writes Brother Sylvester, "Confrater Gabriel was already sick, though not obliged to keep to his bed, yet he regularly followed all the community exercises." Even during his last illness when he was greatly enfeebled, he insisted on making the spiritual reading at the time appointed by the rule; and when at last his strength failed, he begged one of his companions to read out loud for him.

The due observance of religious silence is perhaps one of the most difficult of rules, and the one most easily broken.

Experience teaches that the manner in which either the individual religious or the whole community stands in relation to this point, fixes the degree of regularity for the rest of the observance. There are places and times determined by rule, in which "no one will be allowed to speak without necessity; if necessity require it, it must be done in a low tone of voice." Such is the law which is substantially the same in all regular communities. Our Gabriel was never known to fail in this respect: "I will not break silence without real necessity," was one of his resolutions. In the dormitory and the choir, he was especially careful, for in these places, says the rule, silence shall always be kept. If he had to deliver a message to one of his companions who happened to be in one of these localities, Gabriel would beckon him aside to another place before saying a word. When there was some permission to be asked, or some difficulty to be submitted to his director on the eve of communion-day, in order to keep the strict silence that commences after night-prayers, he would foresee the necessity and provide for it, by going during the day. Were he, however, prevented by circumstances from so doing, and was therefore obliged to delay till after the rosary, he would lay the matter before the superior in the fewest words, spoken in a low tone of voice, and then retire. Nor did he limit his exactness to the hour of strict silence: at all times he was careful on this point, nor would he out of recreation say anything, unless it were in some way necessary. For instance, in school he spoke only of what referred to his studies, accounting it a fault to bring up irrelevant matters at such a time and place.

We have emphasized Gabriel's observance of silence to give the reader an idea of the carefulness with which he kept his rule: but what we say on this particular point, might be extended with equal truth to every other part of his religious life. Even in the smallest detail of his rule he saw the *will of God*: therefore did he strive to conform thereunto in the most perfect manner. His very soul was in maintaining the observance; he set about the performance of his every duty simply to honor and glorify his God, to prove his love for Him, to offer Him some reparation for the countless offenses of men; these and similar intentions, he constantly made use of to maintain his fervor, to show his thankfulness for past graces and deserve new ones. What more is needed to demonstrate the sanctity of this servant of God? "Give me a religious who observes his rule perfectly," said the illustrious Benedict XIV, "and I would be willing to canonize him even during his lifetime."

Let us consider the religious life of Gabriel more in detail. "I will not neglect any of my spiritual exercises," he wrote in his little book, "I will give to each its allotted time, and if unable to attend to it when I ought, I will supply for it afterward." But he was not satisfied with mere punctuality: he performed all his religious exercises, whether in community or in private, with a devotion that was apparent in his deep recollection, and lively faith. It was easy to see that he realized God's holy presence, that he remembered that he was treating with the Divine Majesty; hence there was no distraction, no wandering of his mind, no carelessness in his manner or posture. As the ecclesiastical year unfolded the amazing mysteries of our faith to his view, he apprehended them as living realities, as though they were then actually happening. He prepared for all the festivals of holy Church with faith and love and joy: but to form any adequate idea of his disposition, F. Norbert assures us it would be necessary to have seen Gabriel at such times, and be animated by a spirit of faith and union with God equal to his own. His companions particularly remarked that he spent his last Christmas on earth in such extraordinary recollection, and was so penetrated with the greatness of the mystery, that he seemed wholly absorbed in God.

Owing to our custom of chanting the whole divine office in choir, there is but little room for singularity of devotion, or even for individual notice at all, since the lines in which we stand before the lecterns (or reading desks) cut us off almost completely from each other's observation. Many of our good lay brothers, however, having excellent opportunities of observing the conduct of the priests and students, have testified what they daily saw of the devotion of the young servant of God. Brother Charles thus deposes: "I saw him always recollected in prayer, and his demeanor itself was enough to inspire one with piety." "I can certify," writes Brother Sylvester, "that his whole manner during prayer showed the liveliness of his faith, the firmness of his hope, and the warmth of his personal love for God." He himself when speaking of the midnight office of Matins and Lauds, often said: "When the world is buried in sleep, how beautiful is it not for us, to watch with the angels, and with them sing the praises of God."

His devotion was no less striking when necessity or sickness obliged him to say the office in private. He would insist on saying it standing, with his head uncovered: he would have said it on his knees, if obedience permitted. Moreover, he recited it with such attention and interior devotion, that he spent therein the same amount of time as the community did in choir. And be it remarked, that all this is the more extraordinary, as our students are obliged to recite the canonical office only through rule, which does not bind under pain of sin.

His devotion was likewise displayed in the manner in which he discharged his office as sacristan. It belonged to him to see that everything pertaining to the immediate worship of God was scrupulously clean and in its place. He was exceedingly diligent in maintaining the highest degree of cleanliness and order, both in the church and sacristy. The altar-breads, for instance, had to be literally perfect: a defect which no one else would notice, was enough to make Gabriel discard them. "On this point," says F. Norbert, "I had to mortify him more than once, because he was really excessive in his requirements." It has never been the tradition of the congregation to observe religious poverty at the expense of our Sacramental king, around whose tabernacle we are taught to offer of our best: before the *real* Presence, *sham* wax, *sham* flowers, and *sham* gold are strangely out of place; yet, even in a place where the holiest traditions are daily reduced to practice, Gabriel distinguished himself by constant, supernatural and quite unusual devotion.

16 His Regularity

"A soldier's first duty is to obey his commander," said General Grant, on taking command of his troops; "therefore I shall expect my orders to be obeyed as exactly as if we were on the field of battle." And his obedient men followed the hero to victory.

Now, every religious order is an army, the army of the Lord of Hosts. For the soldier in camp, every hour has its appointed duty: each move and action of the day is made known by the sound of the bugle; even so, religious regularity is the counterpart of military discipline: every action of the observance is made known to the community by the sound of the bell, which thus becomes the call of duty. The regularity thus produced and maintained is the life-spirit of the religious body; without it, all fervor would be but spasmodic, and relaxation would soon paralyze the usefulness of Christ's spiritual militia. No wonder then, that to a religious who has the spirit of his state and the love of his institute, the observance grows dearer as he advances in years, and he realizes the more his responsibility of handing it over unimpaired to a younger generation. Judged even by those who were the most exemplary religious in the various communities in which he lived, our Gabriel was acknowledged as a faultless model. He submitted so heartily to all the prescriptions and signals of the regular observance, that they seemed to have become for him a second nature. He would immediately interrupt whatever he was engaged in, as soon as he heard the community-bell, and would go at once where obedience called him. At the public acts of the observance, he was always the first. When it was his turn to ring the bell, the first stroke of the clock would find him at his post, rope in hand, ready to discharge his duty.

Such indeed was his punctuality and exactness, that no one could rival him: hence whenever one was needed to look after some office or regulation that required particular fidelity, Gabriel was the one generally selected. "Under this head, I remember," writes F. Norbert, "that when we belonged to the community living at Isola, we used to go down to the lower choir in summer for mental prayer. Either through negligence, or the difficulty of hearing the clock at such a distance, it often happened that the religious charged with the little bell, would fail to ring it: so F. Rector ordered Confrater Gabriel to attend to it; from that time on, the signal was never once omitted."

Little by little, his solicitude and punctuality with regard to the observance became such a habit, that even in time of sickness it would give him great concern; and frequently would he remind his attendants of the hour, lest perhaps the bell might not be rung in time. During his last illness, it was he who notified his companions, who were watching in his cell, that it was time to ring for Matins (at midnight); and he kept up his solicitude, even after he was too weak to hear the striking of the community clock. Dear youth! he never shrank from duty, nor did he throw upon another any burden that he could possibly take upon himself: yea, whenever the Rector gave any directions regarding the students, Gabriel would take it as addressed to himself, and diligently perform whatever had been enjoined.

The daily routine of the Passionist life is described as follows in one of Gabriel's letters to his brother Michael, who had asked for a detailed account. "In the evening, earlier or later according to the season, we go to rest, and after five hours' sleep we rise about midnight to chant in choir the office of Matins, which takes ordinarily an hour, after which we apply to mental prayer for half an hour. We then go to bed again for three hours in winter, and two and a half in summer. Rising in the morning, we go to choir to chant Prime and Terce, followed by an hour of mental prayer, and the slightest little collation.[16] Then for two hours and a half we apply to study; then spiritual reading for a quarter of an hour, on the conclusion of which, each one walks by himself through the grounds for half an hour: then to choir for Sext and None, after which comes dinner. Next follows the recreation for three-quarters of an hour, succeeded by a siesta. Then at the sound of the bell, we rise for Vespers, and spiritual reading in common. After this, we apply again to study as in the morning, for some two hours or so, which being terminated, there is half an hour's walk. On Thursdays and all festivals, there is no study in the afternoon, but recreation all the time after Vespers. The walk ended, we chant Compline, have an hour of mental prayer, and then go to supper. When supper (or collation, three days a

---

[16] Editor's Note: A collation is a small amount of food taken on fasting days.

week) is ended, we have three-quarters of an hour for recreation, followed by the rosary and night-prayers. Thus, with joy, swiftness and good-will the day comes to an end."

"O! how pleasant it is," said Gabriel, on another occasion, "to lay one's self down to rest, with the consciousness of having served God (however unworthily) during the whole day!"

"Let the brethren," says the rule, "study to spend piously the time that remains from the common exercises or particular offices of charity toward their neighbor. Let them love silence, and fly idleness." Confrater Gabriel understood practically the importance and extent of this principle: he lost no time. "He was always busy either in his spiritual exercises, or his studies, or in the offices confided to his care: whenever a chance spare moment happened, he employed it in vocal prayer, or interior communion with God." (Process, Sect. 80.) Even during his recreation he was always engaged in some of those light manual occupations, common enough in so many fervent religious communities. "Shun idleness," Gabriel wrote to his brother who had been ordained a priest, "shun idleness, apply to study, labor for God; because this is not the time for rest but for work, above all for a priest." We may best conclude this chapter with one of Gabriel's resolutions, one that gives us the key to all his regularity. "I will be punctual. I will obey the sound of the bell as if it were the very voice of God." Thus did he interpret the saying of the Master: "Blessed are they who hear the word of God, and keep it."

17 His Spiritual Courage

"Man's life upon earth is a warfare," says holy Job, and the victory cannot be won, but by a fierce and constant struggle. Upon every good Christian therefore devolves the obligation of "fighting the good fight" as a soldier of Christ, and displaying and exercising the warrior's chiefest virtue, true moral courage, or fortitude.

After our young hero had resolved to walk in the footsteps of a crucified Redeemer, how many struggles must he not have had to sustain, during all the remaining years of his life! yet, never for a moment did his courage falter or his resolution waver: with rare magnanimity he persevered in the practice of every virtue becoming to the religious state, up to his last breath. True, this magnanimity is to a certain degree common to all religious, inasmuch as it is implied in the religious state itself; but it was intensified in our Gabriel by the fact that he ever sought to realize that immolation, not only in its substance, but constantly strove day by day, and hour by hour, to perfect its spirit in his own soul, by detachment from all creatures and closer union with God. Docile to grace, fearless and undaunted, he withstood and conquered all obstacles from within as well as from without: ever advancing, never pausing for rest on the road he had entered.

"For anyone who has himself set out on the road of spiritual perfection, it will not be difficult to understand from his own experience what obstacles the servant of God had to encounter, so as to maintain that high degree of fervor of life which he displayed even in the novitiate; what violence he had to do to self, what victories to gain over indolent nature, (so inclined to lag in the exercise of virtue), what a manly fortitude and generosity in being faithful on all occasions, without ever growing tepid!" Such are the reflections of his director, and he adds: "In this Confrater Gabriel was endowed with an eminence of spiritual courage that was altogether extraordinary."

We have among his papers some forty of his resolutions: these were written down by him from time to time, but nearly all shortly after his profession. Now these do not at first sight reveal anything extraordinary: both in substance and expression they appear very simple; but what must be accounted as a very rare thing, and a proof of the highest virtue, is that he kept every one of them to perfection. Several of these resolutions have already been quoted, the remainder will be met later on. If the earnest reader desires to gauge the degree of virtue which their observance would imply, let them take up any one or two of them, and try to fulfill them *perfectly* for a single day. He will soon realize the magnanimous constancy and the unusual courage needed in a lifelong fidelity to so many and such difficult promises, covering the whole ground of ascetical theology. By reason of this courageous obedience to grace, he acquired such facility in practicing virtue, that it seemed in him to be quite natural and almost spontaneous. Thus, for instance, to speak to his predominant passion of anger. The reader will remember Gabriel's sensitive and passionate nature; now, listen to Father Norbert: "During the whole time of his religious life, I noticed occasionally that anger seemed to boil in his soul, and would sometimes appear on his countenance, but I do not remember that he even once deliberately seconded its impulses; rather, he was always extremely prompt and firm in keeping it down."

Gabriel's interior struggles, however, were not limited to anger. "In order to remain faithful to God, he had to sustain with regard to every one of the virtues, many combats with the powers of hell; and the struggle was sometimes so obstinate and fierce," says his director, "that he would come to me all woe-begone for assistance. Yet not even once in all his religious life had he to confess a defeat; never did he even doubt of his having resisted with uniform courage and goodwill." Frequently was he tormented with spiritual aridity, darkness, repugnance and various temptations, the latter being at times extremely strong and terrible; still buoyed up by faith, with the sentiments of duty before his mind, he advanced along the difficult path of perfection without complaint or sadness or dejection of soul; on the contrary, he ever maintained such a spirit of generosity and filial confidence toward God, that it seemed as if he did all his duties through natural inclination, accompanied with sensible fervor and spiritual sweetness.

In all his sicknesses and suffering too, he displayed his courage; and though one can offer but a passive resistance to them, for that very reason, there is perhaps no surer or sorer test of consummate fortitude, than the courageous endurance of protracted physical pain, or unreasonable provocation on the part of others. Patience, indeed, hath a perfect work, as the apostle tells us; and according to the wise man, the patient man is better than the valiant. Doubtless in a religious community, where all ought to vie with each other in kindness, there is but little opportunity of practicing patience under persecution; still, there are trials of various kinds allowed by God, to augment our merit and perfect our Christian fortitude. Superiors may seem unreasonable and severe; our work, out of all proportion to our time and strength and ability: add to this, the natural frictions arising from diversity of education and views, characters and dispositions; and maybe too, as in the case of our Gabriel, we have now and then a companion who likes to contradict and annoy us, for the express purpose of testing our virtue. We have already seen with what cheerful patience the dear servant of God would meet these little contradictions:—before his superiors he would humble himself, promising to be henceforth yet more careful to avoid faults, which as a matter of fact, he had never committed:—before his brethren, he would relax into a quiet smile, as if to say: "'Tis all right, go ahead! I know you don't mean it!"

But the beauty of Gabriel's fortitude shone more particularly in the heroic patience with which he bore the painful and lingering illness that brought him to his grave. Oppressed by weariness, greatly inconvenienced by remedies and attentions (that were supposed to give relief), and exhausted by the slow progress of a fatal disease, he yet, as all admit, never uttered a complaint or gave the least sign of annoyance. When questioned as to how he felt he would invariably reply: "Thanks be to our blessed Lord!" "During his last sickness," writes his companion, F. Xavier, "he ever maintained himself in patience and interior peace: he was ready and willing to suffer even more, and gladly availed himself of an opportunity of speaking of the sufferings of Christ and His blessed Mother. He also gracefully submitted to the orders of the attending physician and the direction of his superiors." "One day," says F. Norbert, "I feared from certain contortions caused by pain, that there might be some impatience on Gabriel's part, so I drew near and reproved him with severity, reminding him of the duty of patience, so as not to give the least displeasure to God, or forfeit the merits that we may acquire by courageous resignation. After listening to me with his wonted submission, he said with indescribable confidence and sweetness: 'Be not disturbed, Father, I assure you I am not at all impatient.'"

Confrater Gabriel was not afraid of dying: on the contrary, he longed for it, and when his hour came, far from being disturbed at its approach, he felt such joy and eagerness to meet it, that it became necessary to restrain him. Once, when talking to his companions about his death, he asked, "Do you want me to tell you how I feel about it? Well, I assure you that I am not chagrined at the thought of death; rather, I am afraid lest in the pleasure I feel at the thought of dying, there may be some self-love." And was not the very life he led a continual exercise of heroic courage? Not merely the religious life in itself,—with its essential restrictions and privations and lifelong obedience,—but the religious life as he understood it, a life of complete detachment, of absolute self-renunciation; a life which was a fair embodiment of the three degrees of fortitude: magnanimity, alacrity, and perseverance.

18 His Prudence

Temperance and justice, even when exercised with the greatest fortitude, would not be perfect unless moderated by prudence. Like warp and woof, the cardinal virtues are so interwoven, that the perfect possession of any one of them is impossible without having all the rest; but it belongs preeminently to prudence in particular to combine the remaining cardinal virtues in their due proportion: it is the salt that preserves them intact, as well as the counterpoise that steadies them. If the exercise of all the moral virtues constitutes the perfection of our nature, fortitude is the heart that gives them impulse, while prudence is the head that directs their action.

In general, prudence is the quality by which man chooses the proper means to attain an end; now, as our ultimate end is eternal blessedness with God, prudence teaches us so to dispose of our graces and free actions as to merit everlasting salvation.

This virtue usually takes so long a time to ripen perfectly that it is regarded as properly belonging to old age, of which it is the glory. The experience and reflection which it presupposes, are hardly reconcilable with the ignorance and passions of the young: and it would be all the more extraordinary to find it cultivated, where the danger of its absence is scarcely apprehended. And yet we must fairly reckon Gabriel among the rare exceptions to the general rule, and even admit that he succeeded in practicing prudence in a heroic degree.

We have seen with what consummate tact he won over those who might have thwarted his vocation, or at least delayed his entrance into the monastery, and how he contrived to enjoy his holy solitude unbroken despite their unwise importunities. These sterling qualities of practical judgment and supernatural common-sense (if we may use such a term) did not forsake him in the cloister.

He did not share that rather general delusion of imagining that he would find everything perfect in the religious state, and that everybody in the monastery would be exempt from all the miseries of human nature. Such people are often painfully affected by what they actually find in a religious community: they are scandalized, and are sometimes tempted to regret or to retrace the step they took in leaving the world. Alas! they forget that perfection may be the *aim*, though not the *condition* of every good religious, and that even saints had their foibles and shortcomings as long as they lived.

St. Bernard is reported to have said that if there was any monastery in which there was not a cranky religious, it would be the abbot's duty to send somewhere else to get one; and that he would be worth purchasing at his weight in gold; so great is the good resulting to a community from the presence of such a member, by reason of the virtues he gives occasion of exercising, both in himself and in others. The religious profession does not absorb the weaknesses of our human nature. All those living together in a religious house have more or less to suffer from each other; and he alone has perfect peace who is determined to forget his *rights*, and think only of his *duties*.

"It is no small matter to live in a monastery, or in a congregation, and to converse therein without reproof. Here men are tried as gold in the furnace."[17]

If there is a place on earth where the Apostle's idea of concord is realized, it is in a well-regulated religious community. Here, differences never proceed from malice or hatred, but rather from occasional misunderstandings which do not, on either side, preclude the best of intentions. As a rule the main issue is not a question of charity, but of prudence, or discretion. Now, it is morally impossible on all occasions to be exempt from this failing: at times we can hardly avoid giving offense: for although the members of a community are brought together by a common purpose, and in the main, are honestly engaged in trying to become perfect, yet they ever remain different from each other in temperament and disposition, in age and in education, in talents and in sanctity. Yet, wonderful to relate of a youth, and one of such ardent passions as our hero, Gabriel was never known to have given occasion of complaint to any of his companions, nor to have caused the least displeasure in all his dealings with them. Personally he would put up with any treatment with unruffled and smiling countenance, dissimulating the offense, and as it were, brushing it off quietly. Such was his exquisite tact, his rare prudence, constantly displayed in his daily relations to those in whose society he lived and died. Those who knew him longest and best, both saw and felt that prudence had become habitual with him:

---

[17] The Imitation of Christ, Book I, Chapter 17

his whole conduct was permeated with it; he was never off his guard, never allowed his heart to be surprised by passion, was ever considerate and yielding, never precipitate either in his actions or in his words. His self-possession was particularly remarkable during the scholastic disputations customary among our students. It was a pleasure for his confrères to have Gabriel pitted against them in argument. Others there were as skilled as he in logical wrestling, but none could submit to defeat more gracefully, or show greater generosity in the first full flush of victory. If his opponent, overpowered by the force of fair argument, was reduced to silence, the humble youth took no advantage of his position, but would in a most winning way turn the discussion off to something else. If, in spite of argument and reason, his opponent would not yield, but continued to maintain his opinion with provoking obstinacy, Gabriel would insist no further, but gently broke the discussion off, rather than hurt the feelings of his adversary: prudence suggesting that victory was not to be sought for at the expense of charity. They only who have known by experience the exhilaration and excitement of these intellectual tournaments can realize how easily one forgets himself even in his zeal for truth. "I will repress my eagerness to speak," was a resolution which Gabriel not only wrote with his pen, but which he incorporated into his daily life, and which helped much to his perfection in evangelical prudence.

The cardinal virtue, however, does not wholly consist in regulating our intercourse with our neighbor; it should also shine in the right ordering of our own concerns: and in relation to our Gabriel, we must see how he applied its principles to the proper ordering of his health, his studies and his interior life, subordinating everything to his last end.

No doubt a sensual world would charge him with imprudence in embracing a mode of life exaggerated (they say) in its continual austerity: a contention apparently borne out by Gabriel's premature death. But let all such reflect that it is not mortification, but precisely its absence in the world, that brings to an untimely grave thousands immolated on the altar of pleasure: whereas a severely regulated life is conducive to longevity, as the statistics of religious orders will abundantly show.

Besides, our special mortifications are not left to the caprices of individual fervor, but are regulated by obedience, while even the common exercises prescribed by rule are tempered by the paternal charity of watchful superiors. "Without the superior's permission," the rule says, "let the brethren do nothing under the guidance of their private judgment without the merit of obedience, to which they are specially bound; and sometimes also with the loss of health, with no gain either to discipline or the religious community."

There was then no lack of prudence in Gabriel's manner of life, whether from misguided zeal or transient fervor; neither was he blameworthy on the score of undue application to his studies: for the immoderate vigils and absence of regular recreation, which destroy the constitution of the careless student, are impossible under a wise rule and the vigilance of conscientious superiors.

Health and vigor are precious gifts of God that cannot blamelessly be despised or trifled with: nor was our Gabriel faulty in this particular; for during his religious life he was not guilty of neglect, being always perfectly docile to the directions of those placed over him. And yet after all, supposing our hero to have shortened his days by his fervent life as a Passionist, what follows hence? Is life worth living if it be not consumed in God's service? "Venerable old age is not that of long time, nor counted by the number of years," says the wise man; "but the understanding of a man is grey hairs, and a spotless life is old age....Being made perfect in a short space, he fulfilled a long time; for his soul pleased God; therefore he hastened to bring him out of the midst of iniquities. The just that is dead condemneth the wicked that are living; and youth soon ended, the long life of the unjust." (Wisdom 4:8-9,13-14,16)

We now come to the subject of the literary studies, the purpose of which is clearly outlined in these words of our rule: that, "the young men may become fitter for the care of souls, and may labor with all their strength in our Lord's vineyard": they are often reminded that study is "the special obligation of their state." In a letter to his brother Henry, our Gabriel gives a fair idea of his own sentiments and conduct in this regard. "Apply to study, my dear brother, and believe me that one of the things which frighten me most in having to ascend (if so it please God) to the priesthood, is the thought of how much I should know beforehand. However," he adds, "for the past four years, I have through God's grace applied to my studies a little less negligently than formerly, when I was at home with you."

The truth is that he applied himself with all the ardor of his soul to the mastery of the sciences, especially of philosophy and theology, in order to render himself capable of teaching and preaching to the people the truths of our holy faith, and convert to God the misguided souls of poor sinners. "The servant of God must be ready for every good work," he used to repeat to himself and to his companions, in the words of the apostle (2 Timothy 3:17), to which he would add: "No one can profitably labor in the Lord's vineyard unless he be well provided with holiness and knowledge." Often would he recall with lively feeling that practice inculcated by Ven.[18] Vincent Strambi, that at their studies, the students should imagine themselves surrounded by multitudes of poor abandoned sinners eagerly craving for the blessing of instruction and spiritual encouragement. The fruit he derived from such considerations was evident from his constant and rapid progress in learning. Some of his companions might be accounted more talented than he, but he surpassed them all in diligence and application. In order to lose no part of the time set apart for study, he made it a rigorous law for himself never to leave his room. During the whole time of the lessons, he paid the closest

---

[18] Editor's Note: Now Saint

attention to his teacher, and one could well notice from his deportment that however dry or abstract the matter might happen to be, it penetrated into his very soul. That this was really the case was clearly proven, when it happened to be his turn to unfold the thesis previously explained in school, and prepared by private study; for he would then accomplish his task with such force of argument, handling the whole subject so clearly, that all who heard him were convinced that he had fully assimilated it; and all acknowledged, teacher and class alike, that it was a veritable pleasure to listen to him. Such was his prudent application, in view of his vocation to the ministry; and if God did not commission him to go and bring forth much fruit, neither good will nor earnest labor was lacking in his faithful servant, during all the years of studious preparation. Even when the goal of his ambition seemed at last to fade before him on the distant horizon, and when his health was irreparably shattered, his diligence and attention at school could not fail to strike his companions.

Finally, Gabriel showed his prudence in the manner in which he availed himself of the advantages of spiritual direction. He who does not feel the need of spiritual guidance has not yet entered upon the practice of a true interior life. Difficulties and perplexities occur in which we need counsel and encouragement, and these must come to us from one who is skilled in the ways of the spirit, and can apply this knowledge according to our individual necessities. Those who are wisest and most prudent in directing others have not dared to trust their own lights to direct themselves. "Who is the man that can understand his own way?" asks the Holy Ghost. (Proverbs 20:24) He alone is secure, who acts under prudent counsel, and directs himself by obedience. "He who is his own master, is the disciple of a fool." (Proverbs Ibid.) "Let the brethren," says our rule, "approach their director with confidence, as to a father, make known their wants, lay open the secrets of their hearts, tell him their anxieties of mind, the temptations of the devil and their troublesome thoughts; holding it for certain that as often as they piously do this, they will gain abundant fruits of virtue and seasonable helps from God, and will return not only consoled, but also full of peace and joy."

Our dear Confrater is a living proof of the good results accruing to a soul that is faithful and prudent in its obedience to direction. "It was a consoling task to have the care of Gabriel's interior conduct," wrote F. Norbert. "From his director he kept nothing concealed; he committed his whole soul into my hands:—the thoughts of his mind, his intentions and desires; the affections of his heart and the movement of its passions; his temptations, difficulties and repugnances;—so that his whole conduct, whether interior or exterior, might receive the direction and blessing of obedience. And it was sufficient for me to say just once: 'Conduct yourself in this or that manner': I was certain beforehand that he would do what I suggested, nor would there be any occasion for me to repeat my advice. In the manifestation of his heart, he acted with a simplicity and candor truly worthy of imitation."

The conferences, however, which he had with his director, were not unduly prolonged. The prudent young man would have his questions well prepared, and even written out on a slip of paper. The answer was received without discussion or reply, for he went to seek direction, not to give it; nor did he imitate the conduct of those who try to have their own ways and views approved, and then delude themselves into believing that they are acting under obedience!

One of the signs of an evil inspiration, especially when it is masked under the appearance of good, is that the tempter, "the dumb devil," demands secrecy and silence from his victim. Our Gabriel avoided all these snares by an humble manifestation of all that passed in his interior, and the greater the difficulty he felt, the more resolutely would he conquer self in this repugnance.

"When we consider the whole tenor of Gabriel's life," concludes F. Norbert, "it clearly appears that he possessed the virtue of prudence. He always knew, either by himself or by the advice of others, how to choose and practice the proper means to attain his ultimate end, to avoid the snares and temptations of his enemies, to exercise the virtues, to conquer his passions, and to correspond with God's exalted purposes in calling him to the religious state; and he did all this with alacrity of spirit, sincerity of heart, simplicity and courage of will."

But if we judge from the standpoint of the gospel, the supreme act of prudence in his exemplary life, that one which became the fountain-head of all others, and enveloped them all in its own light and fervor, is the fact that he became a *religious*. "What shall I do that I may receive life everlasting? Keep the commandments. But he answering said to him: Master, all these I have observed from my youth: what is yet wanting to me? And Jesus looking on him loved him, and said to him: One thing is wanting unto thee: If thou wilt be perfect go, sell whatsoever thou hast, and give it to the poor, and thou shalt have treasure in heaven: and come, follow me." (Mark 10:17-21; Matthew 19:17-21) This is the divinely appointed means for attaining evangelical perfection; and Gabriel's supreme prudence consisted in making it the rule of his life. In the prime of life, he saw both the vanity of worldly goods, and the excellence of those of eternity: "he withdrew into the peace of a religious house, embracing an austere life together with the evangelical counsels, in order to attain the more securely his ultimate end"—so says the Official Process.

19 His Spirit of Faith

The presence of grace in the soul is manifested by the practice of three supernatural virtues that spring from grace as from their seed, and are like it and with it, infused into the soul by God's goodness and mercy. These virtues are faith, hope and charity; and they are called theological or divine because they come directly from God, and have Him for their immediate object. The first of these, and the source or foundation of the two others is faith, by which man believes all the truths of God's revelation.

Baptized on the very day that he opened his eyes to the light of the world, brought up under the care of eminently Christian parents; having been taught his first formal lessons in religion by the Brothers of the Christian schools (whose motto is the "Spirit of Faith"), our young hero was no doubt unusually privileged beyond the average Catholic child. This "spirit of faith" communicated to him by his earliest teachers left upon his soul an influence that is traceable in the whole afterwork of his sanctification; it afforded an anchor to his masters at the college to bring him safely through the perilous season of youth, when vanity and passion cloud the mind and heart with dangerous darkness; so that when at last he found himself secure in the harbor of religion, it was clearly seen that an abiding spirit of faith became one of the most striking characteristics of his sanctity. It manifested itself, as many witnesses tell us, in every circumstance, but especially in his conversation. "He was so filled with it," says F. Xavier, "that he would be wonderfully inflamed whenever he was led to speak on religious matters." His joyous submission in believing the mysteries of revealed truth, was plainly noticeable on his countenance, and he had ever ready a collection of little maxims that naturally and appropriately voiced his interior sentiments.

And yet, we must likewise record that our Gabriel's faith was often severely tried by the devil. "Son," says the wise man, "when thou comest to the service of God, stand in justice and in fear, and prepare thy soul for temptation." (Ecclesiasticus 2:1) "Against faith," writes his director, "Gabriel had fierce and protracted temptations to sustain, but he despised them all. They annoyed him usually at prayer. Whatever the mystery might be that he had selected for his meditation, he experienced the most violent suggestions against its truth. But the servant of God would not on this account abandon this holy exercise; rather, he applied himself to it with greater attention of mind, and unswerving loyalty and energy of will. Without excitement or anxiety, he would simply take the shield of faith wherewith he repelled all the fiery darts of the evil one, turning thereby all the attempts of the devil to his greater confusion. Far from suffering from such assaults, Gabriel derived from them an increase of strength: they could only make him cry out all the more fervently in the words of the apostles: 'Lord, increase our faith.'" (Luke 17:5)

Our rule requires us to be men of faith. "In all things let the brethren consider God as present: thus we will pray continually, easily shun vice, and follow virtue." Now, so perfectly did Gabriel carry out this practice, that at all times, and in every place, his mind was filled with the thought of God: nothing could distract him from it: it was his food, his life. So thoroughly had he familiarized himself with it, that his attention to the Divine Presence had become a second nature: whether walking on the public road, conversing with his brethren, or occupied in study or recreation, he kept his mind ever raised to God, and from his countenance and demeanor it was evident that he was engaged in serious thought.

Hence, too, that peace of mind which he maintained under all circumstances, in spite of contradictions, whether from within or without. "I will receive," he wrote among his resolutions, "all things from the hand of God, as sent for my welfare. I will resign myself to everything that happens, be it great or small, by whomsoever, or in what manner soever, it may come about. I will imagine Jesus Himself saying to me: 'It is I that wish it to happen thus,' and I will say to Him, 'Thy will be done'!" Faithful to these resolutions, Gabriel soon acquired the habit of seeing all things *in* God, understanding them to be willed or permitted for his own most holy purposes *by* God, receiving them with all faith *from* God. Thus, too, was he led into that interior life by which he became so remarkable that he might have said with St. Paul, "I live, now not I, but Christ liveth in me": "He dwelleth by faith in my heart." (Galatians 2:20; Ephesians 3:17) For, the more faith is inflamed in a soul, the more God assimilates it to Himself, and makes it work in a divine manner, ever perfecting and increasing therein the strength of all the supernatural virtues. As his director writes: "In conclusion, we may say of this dear and estimable young man, that he lived by faith;" this was especially true of his last years, and in particular, the one preceding his death, when every one of his virtues received an increase and perfection altogether extraordinary and quite noticeable to all.

20 His Lively Hope

When man realizes by divine faith that "eye hath not seen, nor ear heard, neither hath it entered into human heart, what things God hath prepared for them that love Him," then he turns his thoughts and his longings away from the perishable things of earth, and centers them on those of heaven: this is Christian hope. Even as faith makes us judge of all things from the highest standpoint, so does hope raise us far above this earth by desire: as by faith we believe in God as our first beginning, so now by hope we tend to Him as our last end. It is hope that comforts us in our trials, lifts us above our contradictions, excites us to greater efforts; it becomes the soul of fortitude, it animates to magnanimity, to courage in the performance of duty, to patience in enduring, to constancy in persevering.

Gabriel's confidence in God was unlimited and unshaken, it kept him always tranquil in mind: it made him almost actually certain of his future salvation; for he seemed to have no more doubt of being everlastingly happy in the possession of God, and endowed with eternal happiness, than he had of his mortal existence. His director testifies that the virtue of hope in his saintly young charge was of so singular a character, as to seem to him inexplicable. That painful doubt that makes even saints tremble—"shall I be saved?"—did not frighten him in whose heart was an unshaken confidence of obtaining everlasting life: and when he was told that his course on earth was well-nigh over, although unexpected, death frightened him not. Rather we must say that he longed to die, by reason of his hope of being inseparably united to God, of being freed from the danger of offending Him, and of being forever in the society of His Queen, the dear Mother of God. This spirit of his hope and trust in God far exceeded that of an affectionate son for his earthly father. His condition in life did not indeed subject him to those extraordinary trials which we read of in the lives of so many of the saints; yet Gabriel was not exempt from the temptations so often used by the infernal enemy, to destroy or at least to diminish so comforting a virtue in our soul. In this, however, the devil never succeeded: on the contrary, such temptations defeated their own purpose; for the holy young man not only resisted and conquered, but waxed stronger in hope, and perfected his filial confidence in God. There were, to be sure, suggestions that occasionally clouded his soul for a season, and shook his heart with fear:—the remembrance of the faults he committed before his entrance into religion, the knowledge he had of his personal unworthiness, the inscrutableness of God's judgments, the fear of failing in fidelity, and other reasons;—yet like the frightened child that takes refuge in the bosom of his mother, and there finds security and assurance, so did Gabriel in those moments of fear, promptly fly to the loving heart of God, and sweetly nestled there. He did this with such fullness of love, such artless confidence, such abandonment in God's merciful goodness, that his interior peace was quickly restored; and once the struggles were over, there remained not the least vestige of uncertainty or doubt. He frequently recalled to his mind those sentences of holy Scripture that speak of hope and trust in the Lord; he reminded himself that hope is a strict command; he reflected upon the infinite goodness of God, His loving heart, and the pleasure and honor we give Him by cultivating sentiments of confidence in Him. He was wont to encourage himself to hope by saying: "If God has done so much for me as to give me His own Son, what is there I ought not to hope for from Him." "If Jesus Christ became man, and actually died on the cross for me, can I possibly fear that He will not do the rest?" "Were our salvation in our own hands," he used also to say, "we would indeed have reason to fear; but it is in God's hands, and in good hands: let us then trust in God: let us hope in Him."

We can hardly conclude this chapter without remarking, that as Gabriel's heart was filled with supernatural hope, he had likewise a marvelous talent of instilling the same convictions into others. "If he happened to see a companion manifest anything akin to diffidence, or excessive fear, about the interests of his soul, or anything calculated to contract his spiritual growth, Gabriel was at once fired with charity and zeal, inspiring the faint-hearted with greater confidence and courage. And I can attest from personal observation," concludes his director, as well as from the testimony of his companions, "that the supernatural hope with which they were animated in the divine service, was largely due to the words and example of their dear Confrater Gabriel."

21 His Ardent Charity

"By this, all men shall know that you are my disciples," says the Lord, "if you have love for one another;" but to excel in this virtue is confessedly no easy task. Let the gentle reader consult his own heart, and compare its innermost promptings with the standard set up by St. Paul when he wrote: "Charity is patient, is kind; charity envieth not, dealeth not perversely; is not puffed up, is not ambitious, seeketh not its own, is not provoked to anger; thinketh no evil, rejoiceth not in iniquity, but rejoiceth with the truth; beareth all things, endureth all things." (1 Corinthians 13:4) In order to assimilate perfectly this divine virtue, Gabriel labored continually with mind and heart, especially during the time of meditation, proposing to himself the most powerful motives for its perfect practice; drew up rules for his own conduct, foresaw and provided for contingencies, so as to be ready on every given occasion. We may here cull some of those resolutions for our edification and encouragement. "I will not speak of the faults of others, even if everybody knows them already; nor will I show any sign of disesteem for them, either in their presence or behind their back. I will speak of everyone with great regard." "I will try not to provoke anybody by using sharp words, nor will I speak in such a way as to make one feel bad." "I will shut my heart against anything like anger, displeasure or chagrin: much more against every movement of envy or revenge." "I will rejoice at others' success: any feeling of envy I will reckon a fault." "I will practice charity and kindness, especially in my actions, assisting, serving and pleasing my brethren. My answers must be meek, my words mild, my manners agreeable. I will shun altogether particular friendships, so as to offend nobody."

Loving all with an equal affection, he yet delighted in the company of the lowly. He showed no preference for the society of those whose talents were most congenial to his own, but rather to those who were less endowed. He gracefully accommodated himself to their tastes, sympathizing with their feelings and inclinations, for he "sought not the things that were his own," but "made himself all things to all:" —hence the good lay brothers felt themselves perfectly at home with him. In the words of F. Germanus, "nature and grace combined in Gabriel's heart to make of him one of those entirely lovable characters, which are only too rarely met with here below." "We all noticed in him a singular kindness and concern for his brethren," writes F. Francis Xavier. "If anyone fell sick, Gabriel at once volunteered to wait upon him; if he noticed anyone in trouble, he showed his anxiety to comfort and console him. Furthermore, Gabriel's tenderness for his neighbor had nothing sensuous or worldly about it: it proceeded from principles purely spiritual, and manifested itself even in spite of natural aversion. If the superior had sometimes occasion to penance one of the religious," writes this same witness, "Gabriel would interest himself in favor of his brother, and give himself no rest until he obtained a dispensation for him: when, however, the superior was unwilling to let the fault pass unpunished, Gabriel would offer to bear the penalty himself. This often happened, especially in the case of the younger members who had but recently entered the novitiate."

Later on, too, all his companions acknowledged that Gabriel never denied or even put off any appeal for assistance; as soon as the request was made, leaving his own work aside, he would at once charitably help his brother. More than this, he would try to foresee the necessities of his companions, and without waiting to be asked, he put himself at their service. He was faithful to the very letter as well as the spirit of the gospel advice: "Give to him that asketh of thee, and from him that would borrow of thee, turn not away." (Matthew 5:43) "Many a time," writes his director, "in order to moderate his excessive desire to be serviceable, I sent him away with some mortifying retort. 'You are a regular busybody,' I might say; 'it wouldn't hurt you to mind your own business.' Then Gabriel would feel hurt, not at being snubbed, but because a chance to help somebody was denied him." Of a truth, the rule of his life was not the uncharitable maxim of the world: "Let everybody look out for himself!"

We have shown elsewhere, how from his very childhood the venerable servant of God was filled with a tender compassion for the poor of Christ: this ever remained one of his characteristic traits. "He rejoiced," says one of his first biographers, "that although the congregation of the Passion lives on the voluntary offerings of the faithful, we have always been liberal in giving to the poor." "Let the rector," says our rule, "be full of charity toward the poor and toward strangers." And again, "if, after the wants of the houses and churches of our congregation have been supplied, there be any surplus, let it be given to the poor."

"I remember once that when we were going out for a walk," says one of Gabriel's fellow-students, "we found a poor man at the gate who was waiting for a piece of bread. Standing at the porter's side, he jokingly said to the brother: 'I want to see your generosity this time;' and as the slice looked rather small, Gabriel said with astonishment and pity: 'Poor man! why, that bit is not enough to reach his stomach!' The duty of distributing alms usually devolved on this brother, and to urge him to be liberal Gabriel often said to him: 'When you want to give something, let it be something worthwhile:—and be sure to give it with a good heart!' Habitually he stinted himself at table in order that there might be wherewithal to assist the needy. He did not believe in leaving on his plate simply what he did not want himself; but from the beginning of the meal, he deliberately set aside what was most palatable, and would justify the custom to his companions by saying, 'the poor deserve the best morsels: why should we leave only the worst?'"

"Sometimes," writes F. Norbert, "when we were resting on the road from our walk, if a beggar chanced to pass by, Gabriel would ask leave to speak to him. He profited by such occasions to teach the poor how to bear the burden of their misery: he would inculcate a filial devotion to the Madonna, he would remind them that the Son of God chose to be poor, and to submit to all the inconveniences of poverty; he urged them frequently to remember the passion and sufferings of Jesus

Christ; he spoke to them of the great reward prepared for the sanctified poor in heaven; and thus, having comforted and encouraged them he dismissed those unfortunate beings, whose souls were perhaps more famished than their bodies." In his letters, too, he frequently pleaded the cause of the poor, asking his good father and the entire household, to be generous in their behalf. In these appeals we find the following sentiments: "Rest assured of this, my dearest father, that charity never impoverished anyone: on the contrary, the blessing of the poor will call down upon you and the whole family, the blessing of heaven." "Jesus Christ has told us that whatever we do for the poor, He considers as done for Himself." "One of the greatest consolations at the hour of death will be to remember that you never sent the poor away from your door empty-handed."

"To sum up in a few words all that might be said on this subject, Gabriel's charity was universal and inexhaustible, and was truly habitual. To the full extent of his power, by deeds, prayers and words, he strove to encourage the needy, comfort the afflicted and assist the poor. Affable and kind to the extreme, doing good to all, making himself useful to all, the servant of God showed a charity of such a character, that it may be held to have been heroic." Such are the concluding words of the compendium of the Official Process, in its chapter on Gabriel's charity for his neighbor.

22 His Love of God

"Thou shalt love the Lord thy God with thy whole heart, and with thy whole soul, and with thy whole mind. This is the greatest and first commandment." (Matthew 22:37-38) The observance of this law constitutes our essential perfection: all else is but accidental. Temperance, justice, fortitude and prudence: yea, even faith, hope and charity for the neighbor have no supernatural merit save what they derive from the love of God. "He that loveth not abideth in death." (1 John 3:14)

But how can we ever succeed in describing the ardor of Gabriel's heart in its love for God? If he so tenderly cherished his neighbor for God's sake, how much more ardently did he not try to love God for his own sake?...His heart was ever occupied with God, breaking out unceasingly in aspirations of love, now to Jesus in the Blessed Sacrament, now to the Blessed Virgin. During the domestic offices (sweeping and dusting the house), in his studies, conversations, walks, everywhere and at all times, his heart gave way to burning affections for Jesus and Mary: yea, they were the objects around which his fancy played in dreams.

Of course, the enemy of the human race could not bear to see a soul so utterly rapt in God, and he strove to prevent the young student's continual growth in holiness. "There was especially one time," says his director, "when the devil became so furious, and assailed him with such vehemence, that Gabriel suffered indescribable agony. He annoyed him with such abominable suggestions against God, he urged him to utter against the divine majesty such diabolical blasphemies, that he felt the greatest repugnance in giving me even a hint of their nature, and was rendered almost breathless through horror, when speaking of his terrible struggle. The evil spirit however was signally defeated by our young hero: all his attacks only rendered Gabriel dearer to his God, whom in spite of all temptations, he loved daily more and more."

To enkindle this sacred love in his heart, Gabriel used to recall the many blessings and graces that God had bestowed upon him; he contemplated the divine goodness and mercy in his regard, he humbled himself, he urged his heart to an ever-increasing love, he encouraged himself to greater fidelity, no matter what temptations or difficulties should be encountered. The whole world was for him a ladder by which he easily ascended to the Supreme Good, admiring His perfections, His love for us, His more than motherly care for us. Everything that he saw, from the wild flowers of the field to the stars of heaven, were as so many mirrors in which he beheld the manifold perfections of God. Nor was it only from external nature, but from any circumstance or event whatever, he would naturally draw some reflections that helped him to raise his mind to God, and to direct thither the hearts of his companions also. This exercise became so habitual and familiar to him, that all things made his thoughts and affections rise spontaneously heavenward.

Such love could not long be concealed: "can a man hide fire in his bosom, and his garments not burn?" (Proverbs 6:27)

From the very beginning of his life in the cloister, his companions remarked his extraordinary fervor. His prudent superiors counseled him to watch and check this tendency of making public the secret of his soul, and the obedient youth, whose docility kept pace with his fervor, succeeded in controlling the flame that burned in his heart. But at times, during mental prayer for instance, when he ceased to advert to the presence of others, he forgot himself, and despite his good-will, could not help betraying his mighty affection by ardent sighs and aspirations.

He continually spoke of God: for out of the abundance of his heart, what else could he speak of? and "when he was once started on such a topic, his impetuosity was remarkable," says F. Xavier. "It was necessary to restrain him; and sometimes our director would mortify him, calling him a 'busybody,' and one who only wanted to monopolize the conversation, preventing everybody else from saying a word. Yet, the evident sincerity of his conversation never proved unwelcome to his hearers, their own fervor made them delight in all he said, and drew them as it were irresistibly on to follow him."

It is no wonder that one who loved God so much, and with so absorbing an affection would desire to die. If he found it so delightful to commune with his God even here on earth, he was naturally filled with an ever-increasing desire of contemplating and possessing the Supreme Good without fear of separation. From the days of his novitiate, he was anxious to die: he used to entreat our Lord to that effect, with most fervent prayers; and such was the ardor of his desire that his director began to fear lest he should be heard all too soon for the edification of the religious community that gloried in possessing such a young seraph. But though great was his desire to go to heaven, greater still was his submission to the will of God; and often would he repeat with inimitable earnestness: "May the most holy, adorable and amiable will of God be ever done, by all creatures." Steadily, however, the interior fire of divine love became so ardent, that it was slowly consuming the weak frame that was its earthly furnace, and when the supreme hour came at last, we may say with Cardinal Parocchi, that "it was the vehemence of divine love, rather than any corporal sickness that snapped the frail bond that kept his soul here below, and permitted it to unite itself eternally to the one object of its affectionate longings."

There was, however, one great compensation for his exile, one anticipation of future glory, one secure pledge of heaven: the Sacramental presence of Jesus Christ in his church, and as God's infinite love is concentrated in this wonderful sacrament, so all the love of Gabriel's life was centered in the tabernacle. He reckoned himself fortunate in being allowed to spend regularly between five or six hours daily before his King, chanting the office, or silently communing with Him in mental prayer: not only this, but being permitted to receive his Lord thrice a week, and on all feast-days; being able to come and kneel in the Adorable Presence any hour....What a life for one who loves God! Even to the fervent community of which he was a member, Gabriel's devotion to the Blessed Sacrament was an object of admiration. "What I can remember and testify," writes his director, "is far less than was the reality." He was truly enamored of his sacramental Lord. He would often converse on this topic to his companions, and his words were as fire, enkindling in the hearts of those that listened to him, a flame similar to his own. It is impossible to express the deep feeling with which he spoke of the goodness which Jesus manifests, in dwelling among so many souls that are cold and indifferent toward Him, who care next to nothing about Him; in remaining in so many unadorned and unbecoming places, without even that poor little lamp to do Him homage, or keep Him company! Such was his emotion on these occasions, that his eyes would fill with tears, and such his language that all who listened to him were deeply affected. As often as was at all possible, he visited his sacramental Love, and knelt before Him in rapt adoration. "During those visits," says F. Xavier, "he used to be so absorbed in prayer, that we had to shake him in order to draw his attention to something else." He had the habit of going to the choir a little before the office commenced, so as to enjoy the society of his Beloved a little longer than the community. Whenever he had any spare time, even were it only a minute, he would spend it before the tabernacle. In passing near the choir, if he could do it without being noticed, he always genuflected in the direction of the Blessed Sacrament; but sometimes it would happen that his watchfulness would be eclipsed by his fervor, and so his companions were witnesses of many an act of reverence that he never intended them to see. When duty hindered him from actually visiting our Lord, he then visited Him in spirit: quite frequently too, he would ask his guardian angel to go and adore their common Master, especially in the places where He was most abandoned. To his companions he recommended these practices, and he would add: "At the hour of death we will be able to say, 'My Jesus, I paid you ever so many little visits: do not abandon me now, O Jesus, my Love!'"

Now, love is by its very nature unitive, it transforms a soul into the object of its affection; hence in a soul that loves God wholly, God becomes its life, as the apostle says: "He who adheres to the Lord is one spirit." This is the highest stage of the spiritual life, the life of union. For this we have to overcome the evil that is in us by penance, humility and mortification: for this have we to develop the good that is in us by ever-increasing faith, hope and charity: all this prepares us for the last and perfect state, that of intimate union of our soul with God. Though we can never deserve so great a favor, we may nevertheless dispose ourselves for it by the exercises of the purgative and illuminative states, waiting in all humility and faithfulness until the Master bids us "come up higher." Thus, at last there comes a time when God takes complete possession and control of our mind, enlightening our understanding with the light of His presence, and directing *our* will by the influence of *His* will, so that the former becomes the docile instrument of the latter. In this new state, the intellect so lives in God that even in the midst of distracting occupations, it remains conscious of His presence, while the will becomes so united with God's will that it ceases to desire anything whatever save God's good pleasure; "whether we live, or whether we die, we are the Lord's." One's passions indeed may still rebel, but they disturb the mind no longer; temptations may be experienced, but they do not move the will; the night of aridity may sorely try the faithful heart, but it cannot blot out the brightness of that light wherein the soul basks at the feet of God.

This exalted state of union is usually granted only after long years of purification, labor and fervor; but it was bestowed upon Gabriel after a few years of his religious life, and it continued ever to increase unto the full light of glory. If at any time he were suddenly to be asked of what he was thinking, he could have answered: "God!" Never did he entertain willingly any other thought; and as soon as such presented themselves, he banished them. All this was accompanied by the affections of his heart, so that he found therein such nourishment and satisfaction that his interior peace and joy were reflected in his whole external appearance. "As the result of this interior union of love," F. Norbert continues, "he kept his heart fixed and absorbed in God even while engaged in bodily work, the one helping instead of hindering the other, in a wonderful manner. Whether at study or recreation, whether walking alone or in company, whether in school or in choir, he was uniformly recollected and united with God in the superior part of his soul." Consequently when entering on his spiritual exercises, there was no need for him to make any preparation or introduction, for in truth his prayer was unbroken. "His heart," F. Bernard writes, "was in continual activity: at all times there sprang up in him a succession of holy thoughts and burning affections. Always modest and recollected, it seemed as if there was nothing in this visible world that concerned him, or deserved his attention." "He experienced greater ease and relish in communing with the Divine Majesty than others find in the most congenial occupations; whilst contrariwise, for him to turn his mind away from God and holy things, was practically impossible. God had become his life, because He had become the one object of his love; and the peace of heaven that surpasseth all understanding so possessed his heart and mind that he often said: 'My life is full of joy: what more can I desire in this vale of tears? I could not be happier than I am.'"

23 The Evangelical Counsels

Hitherto we have followed our dear Brother Gabriel in his gradual progress unto perfect union with God by love: it now remains for us to see by what means he reached such a sublime degree of holiness.

No one can attain that state unless he be detached from the world: "If any man love the world, the charity of the Father is not in him, for all that is in the world is the concupiscence of the flesh, and the concupiscence of the eyes, and the pride of life." (1 John 2:16) In order to make this detachment complete and this freedom unhampered, Christ in His holy Gospel gives the counsels of *virginity* as the means of overcoming the concupiscence of the flesh; *poverty*, the concupiscence of the eyes; and *obedience*, the pride of life. These are not imposed as commands on anyone, but are offered by him to all who wish to become perfect; and it is the irrevocable acceptance of these gospel counsels which constitutes the religious state, and makes it a state of perfection. Since Gabriel's sanctification was wrought in the religious state, we must of course consider how he observed these counsels of perfection; mindful too, that for the religious, these counsels become strict precepts, by reason of the self-assumed obligation of the religious vows.

"He that does not renounce all that he possesses cannot be the disciple of Christ." (Luke 14:33) Detachment of heart from temporal possessions is the necessary condition of salvation, but actual renunciation is the condition of perfection. "If thou wilt be perfect, go sell what thou hast, and give to the poor." (Matthew 19:21) By his vow of poverty, the religious renounces forever the right of lawfully exercising any act of proprietorship for his own personal benefit. Hence he can neither receive nor give, nor dispose of anything without permission, since he has simply the use of what he needs in food, raiment and shelter: he is further more dependent upon his superior even for the use of such things; so that he becomes in reality poorer than the very beggar.

No sooner had Gabriel entered into religion, than he seemed to have absorbed thoroughly the spirit of poverty. Thenceforward there was nothing in his demeanor that perpetuated his former fondness for vanity and show. He was so completely transformed in manner and tastes, that it gave him particular pleasure to wear old clothes patched with many pieces: yet he was never untidy, for in divesting himself of worldly vanity, he was not expected to cast aside that neatness which is the ornament of religious poverty, and that cleanliness which, if not always next to godliness, certainly goes a long way in rendering it attractive. "Poverty," says the rule, "is laudable, but dirt is blamable." In the distribution of common articles of clothing, whenever it was in his power, he would choose the worst; but if he could not succeed herein, he would try to obtain leave to exchange with others, giving the better and keeping the worse. Never could he be induced to keep for his private use, anything that was not strictly necessary. As the Passionist is his own servant, Gabriel kept his cell, and all it contained, scrupulously neat and in perfect order: namely, a small table, two chairs, and a straw bed; but beyond this he wanted nothing, and rigidly excluded everything superfluous. With regard to his books, he would not keep any that had beautiful bindings, no matter how plain they might otherwise be, but he studiously selected such as were well worn. Never could he be prevailed upon to keep in his room any book that was not indispensable for his studies or spiritual reading; and when told that such or such a work might be of real use to him some time or other, he answered that when "some time or other" came, he would ask permission for the book in question. He did not even wish to keep writing-paper, pens or pencils for his own use, preferring to get these things just when they became actually necessary, but he was directed to conform to the common custom, and avail himself of the permissions allowed by the rule.

"I will not take any food outside of the appointed time," we read in one of his resolutions. "I will be contented with what is served, without ever complaining either in word or thought, mindful that I have made a vow of poverty." Faithful to this resolve, he never brought up the subject of food in his conversation, but with a thankful heart partook of whatever was put before him, and daily prayed fervently for our benefactors. "We are poor," he would often say, "and we should demean ourselves accordingly....The poor are so frequently in want even of what is necessary; we too should be willing to put up with our inconveniences gladly....If some poor people had what we have, they would think that every day was a feast: 'Ogni giorno farebbero Pasqua.'" If, while at the common table, it sometimes happened that Gabriel was passed over, and did not receive what had been served to the rest, he abstained from making any sign whatever: he was even anxious that it should not be remarked, doing all in his power lest the nearest religious should perceive it. On the other hand, he was all attention that nothing should be wanting to his neighbors: and if they happened to be neglected, Gabriel would rise from his place, notify the superior, often going himself to the kitchen, and then beaming with joy, would offer to his companion what had been missed. Even in the use of condiments, such as salt or similar things, he was so sparing that his superior had to watch him, and finally had to lay down a rule to be followed uniformly, which of course, Gabriel observed with great docility. In helping himself to bread, he tried to get the broken pieces from the basket; and whenever he could arrange it, always managed to put the loaves before the other religious, reserving the scraps for himself. "Piety with sufficiency," says the apostle, "is a great gain. For we brought nothing into this world; and certainly we can carry nothing out. But having food and wherewith to be covered: with these we are content." (1 Timothy 6:6) "By the favor of Jesus and Mary, I have renounced all things," echoed our Gabriel, "and I could not be more contented than I am." In the practice of poverty, he made himself dependent even in the least things: never did he take the slightest liberty against this virtue; on the contrary, he strove to do with less than he was allowed. Not only was he detached from created things, but also from whatever was assigned for his use: he was utterly indifferent whether his superior changed it for something else, or took it away altogether. With his crucifix before him, Gabriel ever considered Him "who when He was rich, became poor. He considered the great God of Heaven and the Master of earth being born in a stable, suffering hunger and thirst, heat and cold, persecutions and contempt; not having whereon to lay His head, dying naked and forsaken on the cross:" all this stimulated him to walk in the footsteps of the Master, and to imitate the poverty of Jesus Christ.

As we have already spoken of Gabriel's chastity and virginal modesty under the head of temperance, we will pass to the third evangelical counsel: obedience. It is just because this vow crushes out the pride of life—our chiefest obstacle to salvation—and takes away all solicitude about the ordering of our conduct, that obedience is the foundation of the religious life, and the cornerstone of evangelical perfection. "Let the brethren, therefore, of this least congregation take care not only to profess obedience by word of mouth, but let them also display it in a holy way in their actions. When commanded, let them obey promptly, simply and gladly. When called in any manner, to any services or duties, let them immediately fly to the performance." In these lines, the rule sums up the teaching of the ascetic Fathers, as found in substance in the rule of all religious orders and congregations.

Of Gabriel's own views on this subject, we have an exact compendium in the following resolution: "In what relates to obedience, I will be punctual. I will obey the voice of the superior and of the bell, as if they were the very voice of God Himself. In my obedience, I will examine neither the *how* nor the *why*: I will conform my judgment to that of the superior, reflecting that for me the order is from God, and I will say: 'I obey, O Lord, because it is thy will.'"

His fidelity to these resolutions is attested by all who knew him. "One of the most singular things noticed in this young man," writes F. Bernard Mary, "was his submission and docility in all things: and this was the more remarkable in Gabriel, since his most notable fault as a secular had been precisely his ungovernable temper. No sooner had he joined the congregation, than he reformed to such a degree, that he hardly seemed to be himself any longer: the will of his superior, were it only intimated by a sign, was enough to influence him to do whatever was desired."

In these days when the false principles of Protestantism and infidelity have made independence and self-assertion the main features of manliness and character, it may not be easy for the young to see at a glance the nobility of a life of submission. However, to a thinking mind it must be clear, that our reason exercises its highest act, when enlightened by God's truth; so our will enjoys its grandest independence when governed by the divine will. The full liberty of the will is therefore secured by obedience, as the full illumination of the mind is produced by faith. Yet, as faith ultimately requires an act of obedience from our will, so does obedience finally suppose the truth of faith in our intellect, if its greatest excellence is to be realized. When then, a religious voluntarily submits to a superior, commanding according to a rule approved of by the supreme judgment of the Church, he knows that he is submitting to the will of God. And even as a Christian's faith finds an objective infallibility in the teaching of the sovereign Pontiff, in all that pertains to doctrine and morality; so likewise does a religious find in obedience a subjective infallibility in whatever the superior commands within the sphere of the rule. "He that heareth you, heareth me." (Luke 10:16)—Gabriel's director deposes: "No child in its mother's arms could be more tractable than this youth, under the guidance of his superior: for him, the voice of his prelate was the voice of God; and the least desire was tantamount to an order, which he was anxious to fulfill: consequently I had to be very careful in his presence, not to show any sign of desire or inclination, lest he should construe it as a command, and think himself obliged to carry it out."

No doubt the world, and those who are imbued with its spirit, will fail to see the beauty of obedience, when carried to such a degree: still, when did the world ever appreciate the spirit of God?...But such submission is foolishness!...Yes, but it is the foolishness of God, which is wiser than men....It is unmanly!...Oh, no! It cannot be voted unmanly to be subject to God, and to imitate God: rather, it is *divine*! Look at the crib!...consider the cross!...and remember that it is written: "Let this mind be in you, which was also in Christ Jesus...he humbled himself, becoming obedient." (Philippians 2:5,8)

24 His Spirit of Prayer

By the irrevocable obligation and observance of the evangelical counsels, a religious is freed from the world, and is thereby disposed to raise his soul to God by love. Now the actual rising of our soul to God is called mental prayer: *oratio est ascensus mentis in Deum*.[19] From this it follows that a religious will become perfect just in proportion as he habituates himself to mental prayer.

There is nothing on which our rule insists more urgently and repeatedly than this salutary practice, and our Holy Founder never ceased to assert that the spirit of his institute was the spirit of prayer.

Under the direction of his spiritual guides, Gabriel imbibed this spirit from the beginning: it was the exercise of mental prayer that led him securely through the various phases of the spiritual way, bringing him ultimately to that intimate union with God by love that has been already described. "From the first days of his novitiate," writes F. Bernard, "he so fixed his thoughts and affections on spiritual things that it seemed as though they had hitherto been the only things that he cared for: no sooner had he given himself up to the practice of mental prayer, than he was so fully convinced of its advantages that he felt for it an insatiable longing, and found such sweetness

---

[19] Editor's Note: This is a citation from St. John Damascene's *De Fide Orthodoxa*. The author's citation is translated "Prayer is the raising of one's mind to God." The full sentence reads "Prayer is the raising of one's mind and heart to God or the requesting of good things from God."

in this holy exercise, that a whole hour passed by as though it were only a moment. This, doubtless, was a special gift from the Father of lights, from whom descends everything good and perfect, but still, as Gabriel's director observes, it is no wonder that having given himself to God with all his heart and soul, this young religious received in return so sweet and particular a communication from God that on merely commencing his meditation, his mind was flooded with holy thoughts, and his will with holy affections, thus making mental prayer and recollection of spirit his constant delight. With all carefulness then he availed himself of every opportunity of communing with God, spending herein even the scraps of time remaining from his regular employments: and even in these exterior occupations, his mind was so fixed on God that, with his director we can truthfully say that his prayer was twenty-four hours long every day. Without ever growing tepid in this holy exercise, even in the season of aridity, he maintained his love and practice of it his whole life long, and at last obtained the gift of the most elevated kind of prayer."

During his last sickness, he grieved that the pain he felt in his head prevented him from attending to meditation, but he was directed to be content with making fervent aspirations from time to time, offering up his sufferings in penance for his sins; and he gave himself with such heartiness to these ejaculations that sometimes his attendants judged it prudent to moderate his fervor. Above all, did he delight in the time set apart for the formal exercise of mental prayer, experiencing therein as much ease and satisfaction as many others find displeasure and uncongenial effort. Had he been allowed, he would likewise have spent in prayer the hour of the afternoon siesta, so necessary in southern countries. Similarly, he wished to continue his meditation from the midnight office of Matins till dawn, but his constitution and his studies forbade it, and the coveted permission was never granted.

"From the beginning," F. Norbert testifies, "the maxims and mysteries upon which he meditated impressed him so deeply, and so filled his soul with affections, that unconsciously he would break forth into sighs and tears, so that I often reprehended him for distracting the religious who were all engaged together at their usual meditation." F. Bernard writes that during his prayer, Gabriel's appearance was beautiful to behold: he remained immovable like a statue, showing by his evident composure and devotion how deeply all his faculties were immersed in the object of his meditation. "From then on, until God tried him by aridity of spirit," continues his director, "the time of prayer was for him a season of heavenly delights." The time of trial however, came soon, and God left His servant to battle against spiritual dryness and temptation, that his fervor might be proved and tested. "Against Gabriel's spirit of prayer," says F. Norbert, "hell aroused itself, and many were the attempts which the devils made to induce him to give up so salutary an exercise, or at least to make him grow tepid in its practice; so that when prayer-time would come, it seemed to Gabriel that he was going to choir only to be tempted." He experienced the most frightful and violent assaults against the truth of whatever he had selected for his meditation; and at other times, horrible and disgusting imaginations were superadded. But after disclosing all these difficulties to his spiritual guide, Gabriel despised all the artifices of the enemy, persevering with stronger purpose in his prayer, and never desisted from his meditation. These struggles did not even cause in him any undue agitation of soul; he simply and calmly continued his interior communion with God with increased attention, faith and resolution: "so that in course of time," says F. Bernard, "he attained such a degree of perfection in holy prayer, that he could spend the whole time set apart for it without being disturbed by any distracting thoughts."

Our Gabriel however did not attain such a state of continued and elevated prayer without personal exertion. "From his very novitiate," writes his director, " the servant of God strove to dispose himself for the gift of prayer, by purifying his soul ever more and more, emptying his heart of all affections, and disengaging his mind from all thoughts that were not about God or holy things. With great diligence he checked his natural curiosity, curbed his self-love, and avoided all useless thoughts. He was averse to listening to mere worldly news, saying: 'It is useless to spend time in such discourses; after all, what comes of it? Even did it entail no other inconvenience it may prove distracting to us in our prayer.' 'Time spent in talking about such things is time lost: let us rather keep nearer to God.' His aversion for indifferent topics of conversation was so well known to his companions, that if they happened to be engaged on such subjects during recreation, no sooner did

Gabriel join them, than they at once substituted either something devotional, or else some topic relative to their studies. He frequently spoke about mental prayer, and remarked that 'God often inspires us to mortify ourselves in some little thing or other that is retarding our growth in holiness, and if we do not correspond to the inspiration, we do not succeed in our prayer either.'"

He also paid particular attention to spiritual reading, so highly esteemed by the masters of ascetic theology, as an admirable help to meditation and interior recollection, prudently using those books that his director judged best adapted to his spiritual progress. Nor was he less careful in hearkening to the advice of the Holy Ghost: "Before prayer prepare thy soul, and be not like a man who tempteth God." (Ecclesiasticus 18:23) To succeed the better in his prayer, he always chose and prepared the subject beforehand: then, having guarded his spirit with extraordinary care, he entered upon his meditation with the greatest interior relish.

The kind reader must have noticed that when speaking of prayer, we have repeatedly used the word *meditation*; by which we mean the reasoning out of some spiritual maxim or truth of faith. It would be impossible especially for beginners to apply oneself for any length of time to the exercise of mental prayer without the assistance of meditation. *In medita-*

tione mea exardescet ignis.[20] (Psalm 38:4)[21] It is in meditation that the fire bursts out, that is, the fervor of charity. Now, this meditation is a science, the science of the saints, and its principles, rules and methods are learned from accredited masters. Although St. Paul of the Cross has not bound his children to follow any particular method of prayer, a few simple rules are laid down in the novitiate, and these our Gabriel mastered even before he was clothed in the holy habit. Still, after the theory of meditation is mastered, it long remains the most difficult, as well as the most laborious part of prayer; and because they shrink from making the necessary effort, many never become familiar with this holy exercise, which is the royal road unto union with God by love. Not so with Gabriel. He applied to meditation with an earnestness that neither sensible comfort, nor spiritual aridity could relax. He realized that habitual prayer is a gratuitous gift of God; but he likewise knew that the personal labor of meditation is its condition. However, "during the last year of his life, and a little more, I had," says F. Norbert, "to forbid him the exercise of formal meditation, because the manner in which he applied himself thereunto really injured his already shattered health." Some of our readers will easily realize what a sacrifice this prohibition may have been for the fervent youth; still, he obeyed with the docility of

---

[20] Editor's Note: In the Douay-Rheims, this phrase is translated "in my meditation a fire shall flame out"

[21] Editor's Note: The author uses the Latin / Greek Psalm order. This verse is numbered 39:3 when using the Hebrew Psalm order.

a child. It must be remarked furthermore, that this prohibition was laid on him only toward the end of his life, and then only with regard to formal meditation; the habit, however, of interior recollection and communion with God (which is true mental prayer) continued, as we have seen, in Gabriel without interruption, and was exercised by him to the very end of life. We read of the martyrdom of love suffered by St. Aloysius when he was directed to distract his mind from God; such an injunction was not laid on our Gabriel, because obedience to it would have been impossible, whilst the strain of trying to comply with it, would have defeated its object. The object of meditation is to enlighten the understanding so as to move the will to raise itself to God by mental prayer; and since this end was habitually attained by Gabriel, there was no danger in his temporary abandonment of the means, especially under the watchful eye of his director. Besides, the lights which reason derives from the truths of faith by meditation, were now directly communicated to his intelligence; and when speaking of his union with the Supreme Good, we have shown how completely his mind was filled with this heavenly light, and how it gently moved his will to unite itself to God by most fervent aspirations.

25 His Devotion to the Passion

"Let the meditations generally be about the divine attributes and perfections, and also about the mysteries of the life, passion and death of our Lord Jesus Christ, from which all religious perfection and sanctity takes its rule and increase." Such is the commencement of the chapter on mental prayer in our rule.

God himself could find no more excellent way to manifest His attributes and perfections, and above all His love for man, than by the passion and death of Jesus Christ; and man can find no more powerful motive than this to avoid sin, to practice virtue and to love his God.

"The Passion was the ordinary subject of Gabriel's meditations," writes his director; "but he did not rest satisfied with a few superficial considerations and affections; he entered into it in such a manner as to be penetrated with the reasons for which Jesus suffered and died, investing himself with his sentiments and motives, especially his infinite love; and to render these meditations practically useful, he considered in particular those virtues of which our suffering Lord gives us such bright examples, bringing home to himself their circumstances and divine perfection. In the light of these considerations, Gabriel humbled himself for his faults and shortcomings, conceived a high esteem and love of virtue, encouraged himself to practice it, forming at the same time the strongest resolutions. These he carried away in his heart, kept them continually before his mind, and tried to incorporate into his daily life."

Thus the passion of the Son of God became deeply engraved upon his heart, so that a mere glance at the crucifix would instantly recall the considerations, affections and resolutions of his prayer, and thus too, he conformed his life ever more and more to the life of Jesus. *Passio Domini nostri Jesu Christi sit semper in cordibus nostris*: this was his motto, symbolized by the Sign that we wear on our breast. "May the Passion of our Lord Jesus Christ be ever in our hearts!" Truly was it impressed on his! No conversation pleased him if not seasoned with the memory of our suffering Lord, "*Gesu Appassionato*" as the expression runs in his native tongue. Truly could he have spoken of himself in the words of the apostle: "I judged not myself to know anything among you but Jesus Christ and Him crucified." (1 Corinthians 2:2)

"From the commencement of his religious life, when he began to meditate seriously on this subject, the servant of God applied all the powers of his soul to it," so that, as F. Bernard deposes, "it seemed as if his mind could fix itself on nothing else, and as if the love and gratitude of his heart could be centered on nothing else. It was enough merely to allude to Christ's sufferings to make his fervent spirit burst into sudden flame, like flax when touched with fire. He would at once begin to speak with wonderful fluency and enthusiasm, and this he would keep up for a considerable time. At such times our companions, who before had been conversing among themselves, would as by a common impulse turn to Gabriel, and captivated by his extraordinary and touching words, listen eagerly to him as he spoke of our duty of mourning over the sacred passion of Jesus, in union with His Blessed Mother." Often, too, did he call their attention to their distinctive obligation as Passionists "to promote according to their ability, devotion to the sufferings and death of our Blessed Redeemer in the hearts of the faithful." A few times only, he was chosen to deliver a little discourse in the church attached to our retreat, and then he plainly showed to all, his zeal and fervor to the great spiritual edification and profit of his hearers: but it was not often given him to promote this grand work in public, daily however he earnestly besought our Lord to assist all those that advanced this salutary devotion.

Even in His glory, our Blessed Saviour exhibits the wounds He received in His crucifixion as so many trophies of His love, for the contemplation of saints and angels; and such is His desire that on earth too, all men should piously remember them, that He left us the Sacrifice of His Body and Blood as a perpetual commemoration of His death. When assisting at Mass our Gabriel found his delight in devout meditations on the Passion, together with fervent prayers. In his visits to the Blessed Sacrament, and in Holy Communion one thought was predominant in his mind: *"He who is here, suffered and died for me!"* During the hours spent daily in meditation in the shadow of the tabernacle, one thought was ever welling up from his heart: " He who suffered and died for me *is here!*"

The Sacrament of the Altar was then for him truly what Christ desired it to be, the living commemoration of the Passion.

There was yet another means to the same end, dear to the heart of Gabriel; one which the Church of God has ever conspicuously placed both in life and in death before the eyes of her children: the crucifix. "They shall look upon Me whom they have pierced, and they shall mourn;" (Zachariah 12:11) "and I, if I be lifted up from the earth, will draw all things to Myself." (John 12:32) "Whilst they are in their cells," say our regulations, "let the religious keep the crucifix before their eyes, and often take refuge in its sacred wounds and accustom their hearts to send forth frequent darts of love toward their sovereign Good." Gabriel fully entered into the spirit of this regulation; for he kept his crucifix on his table by the side of his book, or even held it in his hand: and so frequently did he press it to his lips, that he actually wore it away. It was principally at the foot of his crucifix that he spent those few minutes of meditation before spoken of; his first thought in the morning was Jesus Crucified; with His image closely pressed to his heart he fell asleep at night; while reciting the divine office in choir he had continually before his eyes a devout little picture of the crucifixion, joined to which was a still smaller one of the Virgin of Dolors. For Gabriel, the crucifix became the book of life; therein he studied the mystery of a crucified God, humility, patience and love supreme; from it he imbibed a preference for poverty, humiliation and suffering, thus "Bearing about in his body the mortification of Jesus." In the words of his biographer, "Gabriel's soul was like an altar on which was continually offered some act of interior mortification or exterior penance," growing thereby into the likeness of Him who was "as a worm and no man, the reproach of men and the outcast of his people." This is the explanation of those excesses and extravagances (as the world would style them) which we adverted to when speaking of his poverty and mortification, his charity and humility, his regularity and obedience. The young worldling of Spoleto had learned from the cross to love and even seek to be despised, that he might the more easily attain to religious perfection. This asceticism, however, is not peculiar to the Passionist rule: it is the pith of all Christian spirituality ever since the days of the apostles. "Let this mind be in you, which was also in Christ Jesus, who being in the form of God debased Himself...humbled Himself...even unto the death of the cross." (Philippians 2:5, 8)

26 His Devotion to Mary

It would seem natural for the kind reader to conclude from the foregoing chapters, that he had formed a fair estimate of the extent and character of Confrater Gabriel's holiness; but the present chapter will, we hope, entirely disabuse him of such an idea: for strange as it may seem, the mainspring of Gabriel's sanctity, its largest ingredient, its master-key opening for us the most intimate recesses of his heart, has not yet been mentioned. Though sanctity is essentially the same in all the saints, yet it assumes in each great servant of God, certain traits more or less clearly defined, that enables the church to sing of him: *"Non est inventus similis illi*: His like hath not been found."

Now, Gabriel's director tells us, that his devotion to the most holy Virgin was his greatest characteristic. So devout was he to Mary, so filled was his heart with love for her, that any description of it would prove inadequate. He does not hesitate to assert, that not only did he never see in anyone else so singular a devotion, but that he had scarcely ever met with anything similar to it even in books; and only in the lives of the greatest saints was its parallel to be found at all. In his supplicatory letter to Pope Leo, Cardinal Parocchi expressly says: "Mary was the very soul of Gabriel's life, the source and model of the sanctity to which he attained; so that it may be truly said, that in his devotion to the great Mother of God, he has scarcely been equaled by any even of the greatest saints.

St. Gabriel Kneeling Before Our Lady of Sorrows

This devotion of his," continues the cardinal, "was evidenced by so many deeds of unusual piety, that it was the belief of those that knew him, that this holy youth had been raised up in the Church by God, to serve as a model of filial love and reverence to all the clients of the most holy Virgin."

Such is the judgment of the illustrious cardinal, after reading the testimony of the official process for Gabriel's beatification; and, be it allowed us to say, that we are deeply thankful to our Blessed Mother for having (besides the many favors received from her merciful hand) deigned to give to our congregation, so dear a servant of hers. Owing its very foundation to the Mother of Sorrows, our little congregation will not consent to be outdone by any other in filial piety and love. "Let them entertain a pious and ardent devotion toward the Immaculate Virgin Mother of God," says St. Paul of the Cross in our rule, "let them strive to imitate her sublime virtues, and merit her seasonable protection amidst so many dangers."

Gabriel's devotion could not but expand under auspices so favorable; and in fact, it was soon an object of admiration to all, and gently stimulated them to greater fervor. Among the saints he honored with especial affection, those who had been most devout to Mary; and among their books he showed a predilection for those that treated of her greatness. Two books in particular were ever dear to him, and served to inflame his piety toward his heavenly Queen: the "Glories of Mary" by St.

Alphonsus, and "The Love of Mary" by Dom Robert, a Camaldolese Hermit.[22] The second of these was his chosen favorite. In the little volume he found his delight: it was, besides, his sure guide in his devotion to the Madonna. Owing to his daily use of it, for the six years of his religious life, he wore the little manual to pieces: he fed upon its pleasant pages with ever renewed fervor.

"After reading these two books," says F. Bernard, "Gabriel's heart became a furnace of love toward the Queen of heaven: his mind was in a manner transformed into Mary, so that he could no longer speak, nor think, nor act, without having her present before his mind."

We may be asked how Gabriel's continual attention to the Blessed Virgin can be harmonized with what has been said about his continual attention to the presence of God.

We must remember then, that in this life we cannot know God essentially, that is, we cannot understand the divine nature, we cannot even see it and live. The majesty of the Most High is revealed to us principally in Jesus Christ, His Incarnate Son: but after His deified humanity, we can arrive at our knowledge of God, His perfections, and His ways, from His works; and amongst them all, from the devout contemplation of the most Blessed Virgin. Is not Mary the Mother

---

[22] "The Love of Mary" has been translated into English, and was published in New York in 1856, by Edw. Dunigan and Bros. A new edition was since put on the market. There are many editions of the classical work of St. Alphonsus. [Editor's Note: "The Love of Mary" and "The Glories of Mary" are both available from TAN Books.]

of Jesus, the Mother of God? Is she not therefore, the masterpiece of an all-powerful, all-wise, and an all-holy God? Is she not the adequate realization of His ideal in the orders of mere nature, of grace and of glory? Even as Jesus is the uncreated and consubstantial image of the Father; so is Mary the created, the subordinate but adequate mirror, of all His communicable perfections. Surely, God owed it to Himself, to make her as worthy of being His Mother, as a created nature would allow of: for anything short of this would not have been worthy of God. Surely the God who is the author of the Fourth Commandment of the decalogue, would Himself show what a loving and all-powerful Son *could do* for His chosen Mother. Therefore, Mary is all that a mere creature could ever be; for theology and common sense teach that even God could not create a higher or holier office, than that to which Mary was predestined. Only one could ever stand in such a relation to the Most High: only one could look with adoring love into the face of her God, and say, "Thou art my Son!"

We need not wonder then, when we are told by F. Bernard, that Gabriel seemed to live and act under the hallowed charm of the Virgin Mary: a passing thought, a casual word about her, was enough to enkindle his devotion, and plunge him into sweetest contemplations of her unparalleled greatness. Whenever he thought of Mary, he most naturally thought of God also, whose mother and masterpiece she is: in a word, he saw God in her, and her in God. In one of his earliest biographers, we read: "After God, the Supreme Good, Mary was Gabriel's life, his sweetness and his hope; devotion to her clothed all his virtues with a new and gracious splendor; and even as the singular graces with which God adorned him were reflected from his countenance, nay his whole demeanor; so too, did it seem that they also reflected Mary's beauty, on account of the continual and tender affection which he cherished for her." So congenial to mind and heart was this exercise, that merely by recommending himself to her by one "Hail Mary," it would have been quite easy for him to spend any hour of the day or night in rapt communion with her: for it never happened that her image was quite absent from his mind. During his novitiate, when the young men were not left free to select their subject for mental prayer, but had to follow the directions of the F. Master, it grieved our Gabriel that he could not always meditate on our Blessed Lady; so, he used to repeat: "Recede a me, Domina: Depart from me, O Lady, depart from me!" "It seemed as if all his thoughts were concentrated on the Madonna," writes his director, "and that his constant desire was to meet her approval; and I must acknowledge that to explain fully how his heart was filled with love for her, would not be possible." During his last illness, on account of his sufferings, it gave him great pain to talk to anyone, or even to listen to others: still, when the subject broached was the Blessed Virgin, then, whether it was that he forgot his sickness, or that he experienced some kind of relief in his sufferings, not only did he love to listen to such discourse, but he would himself take part in it, showing his reluctance to discontinue it at all. He had made it a law to himself, to practice the counsel of St. Bernard: *Non recedat ab ore, non recedat a corde*: Let the sweet name of Mary be ever on your lips, and ever in your heart. He always pronounced it with a reverence and love that showed how deeply it affected him. Sometimes, forgetting the presence of his companions, he would murmur in an undertone: "Maria mia!" and his face would be all lit up with joy. Whenever he heard others mention that sweet name, he would uncover his head, and bending low, would thus salute his Queen. It was from a particular love for her, that he asked to have her holy name as his title, choosing to be called Gabriel of the Holy Virgin of Sorrows. Urged moreover by the ardor of his devotion, he ever sought new means of manifesting his love. Hence, many a time, his director informs us, he pleaded for permission to burn the holy name of Mary into his breast with a red hot iron. This being refused, he proposed what seemed to him very much more allowable: he asked leave to cut the name into his flesh with a sharp knife. Of course such petitions were never granted, but there is no doubt of either the sincerity or extraordinary fervor, which prompted the young religious to think of such very unusual practices.

Even as Gabriel's devotion to our Lord received its special feature from the Passion, so did his piety toward Our Lady take its distinctive coloring from her Compassion. To his heart, Jesus appealed by the greatest manifestation of His love for us: He was *Gesù Appassionato*; so too did Mary appeal to his heart by the greatest manifestation of her love for us: she was *Maria Addolorata*.[23]

---

[23] We have not in English the exact equivalents of these endearing expressions.

No devotion is more pleasing to Mary, than devotion to her dolors. In venerating her as "Our Lady of Good Counsel," "Our Lady of Perpetual Help," "Our Lady of Mercy," etc., we seem to be drawn more by our own interests; at best, we honor her in some one of her privileges and graces: such as the Immaculate Conception, her glorious Assumption, and the like: we share in her joy;—but by devotion to her dolors, we share in her sorrows, we suffer with her, we forget self to compassionate her virginal motherly heart crushed with unutterable grief. In heaven, there is no privilege over which Mary rejoices more than to have shared in her divine Son's passion: nothing for which that loving Son is more grateful, than for her compassion: nor can we do anything more pleasing to Him in our veneration for her, than in sympathizing with her. Besides, for Gabriel, this devotion seemed the completion, the correlative of his devotion to Jesus Crucified, as a Passionist. He was proud of his allegiance to his King and his Queen: Gabriel, the Passionist, under the patronage of the Queen of Sorrows! This double spirit rightfully belongs to us. We see it in the directions for the novices: "You are recommended," we read therein, "to recall frequently during the day, the remembrance of the Passion of our Saviour, and the dolors of His most holy Mother, as the spirit of our institute requires." The rule itself is more emphatic still: "They [the religious of the congregation] should honor with due devotion, the Blessed Mary Mother of God, ever Virgin; have her for chief patroness, constantly commemorate the most bitter sorrows which she suffered in the Passion and death of her Son, and promote her veneration both by word and by example." "Gabriel's devotion to the sorrows of Mary was most tender," writes F. Xavier, "and I think he even felt it more than his devotion to the Passion, or the holy Eucharist:—he spoke of her sorrows very often." "His devotion," says his director, "which, as we have seen, was quite extraordinary, was concentrated in the *Addolorata*. She was his predominant thought, his heart, his all." If during the day he had a little free time, were it never so short, he would employ it in this exercise: and furthermore, he inculcated the same to his fellow-students, in that affectionate and winning way that was his own: "When we have two or three minutes left over from our office," he would say, "how can we use them to better advantage, than in compassionating our dear Mother? Let us not forget her anguish, and at the hour of death, the Madonna will console and assist us: yea, if expedient for our soul, she will show herself to us then, and she will manage that we will not feel the pains of death." Of a truth, these words were literally realized in his own happy passage, for it was like a gentle sleep.

"One Saturday," says F. Bernard, "I asked our dear companion whether he had made his meditation that evening on *heaven*, that being our usual subject for Saturday. 'No, indeed,' replied he; 'my heaven is the dolorous heart of my dear Mother!'" This F. Bernard was second only to F. Norbert, in being the confidant of the secrets of his soul. He tells us that "having applied himself to his meditation on the Passion of Jesus, Gabriel rested therein with all the strength of his mind. But understanding from the beginning of his spiritual career, that this Passion was wholly reflected in the most holy heart of Blessed Mary, as in a mirror; Gabriel then took up his abode in that pure heart of hers, and united with it in compassionating the sufferings of the Divine Redeemer, and in weeping over them. From this, there naturally followed a sentiment of compassion for the sorrowing Mother herself; and this it was that seemed most to affect the sensitive heart of my young companion." Like a traveler selecting his standpoint, from which to study at leisure the details of a vast landscape, Gabriel surveyed the mysteries of the agonizing heart of Jesus, from the vantage-ground of Mary's heart, the dearest and the nearest to Him of all human hearts. Hence, it was *in* that heart, and *from* that heart, and *with* that heart that he henceforth learned to weep over the mysterious abasement unto death, of the Incarnate Son of God: and he saw that the sword that pierced Mary's soul through and through, was none other than the blessed Passion of Jesus. In these meditations, he realized how much he had been loved by her, how much he had cost her, how much he had received from her, and these thoughts, spiritually digested in his heart, made it bleed in sympathy and compassion, his whole life long.

Such then was the special characteristic of Gabriel's devotion; hence, whosoever would be thoroughly acquainted with the sanctity of this dear servant of God must look at him from this point of view: Gabriel of the Sorrowful Virgin. Having consecrated himself unreservedly as the servant, nay, the child of Mary, he ever showed unlimited filial confidence in her patronage. If he happened to find himself in some sudden perplexity, which at the time he could not submit to his director, Gabriel would at once turn to the Madonna, commend himself to her from his heart, and then choose with assurance whatever seemed the best thing to be done. In fact, before beginning any action, especially those of importance, he made an offering of it to his Queen, saying: "O my Lady! holy Mary, take this matter in hand: help me." When beset with temptations, or troubled in any way, he invariably placed himself in Mary's hands: holding it for certain that with her merciful assistance, he would triumph at all times over all his spiritual enemies. It was really touching to hear him in such circumstances, repeating words like these: "O Mary, my mother, you must concern yourself about this affair"; and to restore peace to his soul he would say simply: "O, mamma will attend to it!"

Truly, then, did our Gabriel trust in Mary, even as a child trusts its mother. The last words of Christ on the cross: "Behold thy mother!" were no mere speculation *for him,* because he knew that for Mary, the corresponding words were a reality: "Behold thy son!" In all his dangers, he ran to her with childlike confidence, nor was he ever disappointed. Amid the continual disturbances that raged around our retreat at Isola, during the revolutionary tempest of 1861, he writes thus to his good father, Signor Possenti: "That sweet Virgin of Sorrows who cannot look without compassion upon our misery, keeps us safe enough under her protecting mantle; and the very swords that transpierce her blessed and most pure heart, she uses for our defense." "The passion of Jesus Christ and the dolors of Mary," he used to say, "are the inexhaustible treasures of a good Christian." He held for certain the opinion of St. Bernard, that all the graces won for us by our Saviour, are dispensed to mankind through His Blessed Mother.

But if Mary's dolors were Gabriel's sorrows, her joys too, were his joys; her honor and worship, his ambition. "He rejoiced exceedingly," says F. Norbert, "whenever he heard any extraordinary honor paid to the Madonna, or any remarkable grace obtained through her intercession. On the other hand it made him sad to hear that the great Mother of God was forgotten, that her worship was neglected, and that the irreligious were enraged against her. In his fervor he composed for himself a long series of articles which he styled, 'The Madonna's Credo': it is a cento[24] of the teaching of the greatest doctors and theologians of the Church: it is a crown of praise, in which faith, love and confidence shine like a cluster of brilliants."

So inflamed was his innocent, loyal heart, with the love of his Mother and Queen, that not satisfied with loving her himself, he sought every possible means to make her known, honored and loved by everyone else: nothing short of making her clients be as numerous as all mankind would satisfy him. His zeal on this point was so honest and so constant, that even from the days of his novitiate, he wished to bind himself by a formal vow, to promote devotion to the holy Mother of God to

---

[24] Editor's Note: A cento is a literary work made up of quotations from other works.

the extent of his ability. At first his request was not granted, for a vow is quite a serious thing to undertake; and a perpetual vow may be repented of when it is too late. But Gabriel soon proved beyond a reasonable doubt the solidity of his devotion, and after five years of patient demand and trial, after a thousand tokens of affection and zeal, he was at last permitted in the year 1861, to bind himself by vow to be Our Lady's champion for life. "This he did," says his director, "to the unspeakable joy of his heart, and," (he adds) "to the great profit of his soul." On her part, the loving Mother of men, wishing to testify her acknowledgment of this extraordinary and generous act, rewarded her saintly son with the inestimable gift of never thereafter committing the least deliberate imperfection. Thus it was that the gracious Sovereign who honored Gabriel with a vocation to the religious state among her chosen servants, herself crowned the edifice of his personal holiness, and raised it to the summit of perfection, by the royal favor of being preserved from even the least willful fault.

27 Other Special Devotions

The Church of Christ is now divided into three parts, the church *triumphant* in heaven, the church *suffering* in purgatory, and the church *militant* on earth. Among these three parts, there is an organic unity, with a constant intercommunication of merits and prayers. This mutual participation we profess to believe, under the name of "the communion of saints."

What is more cheering in this vale of tears, than to realize that we are only bodily separated from our departed friends, and that we can make them feel the sincerity and permanence of our affection, by relieving their sufferings, and hastening the time of their deliverance, by means of our prayers and good works, and above all, by the holy sacrifice of the Mass, and the application of indulgences.

Even as a secular, our young hero was noted for his charity toward the faithful departed; and one of his college companions says of him, that among the sodalities and confraternities that were there established, young Possenti was enrolled in such as held out the greatest spiritual inducements, that he might thereby be able to succor the souls in purgatory the more effectually. After entering the religious state, he wrote on one occasion only to his aged father for money, which he begged him to supply in his name in charity for the suffering souls. It seems that he had promised in case he would be judged worthy of pronouncing his vows, at the end of his year of probation, that he would ask his father to make an offering of ten dollars[25] by way of gratitude to the poor souls, to whom he had specially recommended this intention. Then, on the very day of his profession, partly to thank them for their intercession, and partly to secure their interest in his final perseverance, he made in their favor the "heroic act," by which he made a total renunciation of the *satisfactory* part of all his good works, together with a complete resignation of all the suffrages to be offered for himself after death, putting them all in the hands of the Blessed Virgin, the merciful queen of purgatory. "Never in my experience," says F. Norbert, "have I known anyone so anxious and industrious to gain holy indulgences, in order to apply them to the faithful departed. Not satisfied, however, with what he could personally do, he strove to quicken the devotion of others to hasten the deliverance of those prisoners of God's justice. So evident was his zeal in this cause, that his religious brethren surnamed him 'the Apostle of Purgatory.' He nobly endeavored to induce all who came within the sphere of his influence, to make the 'heroic act,' but we cannot say that his efforts were rewarded with uniform success." To some he seemed to be too forgetful of his own interests, over-generous, in fact. His reply on such occasions was: "Charity which makes restrictions is not the right kind of charity." "This is my commandment," says the Master, "that you love one another *as I have loved you.*" Sometimes, when he was pleading most fervently, one of his fellow-students would half-seriously interpose: "Confrater, who will think *of you?*"

---

[25] Editor's Note: This is around four hundred dollars in today's money.

..."Of *me?*" ...he would answer, with surprise—"who will think of *me?* ...Well, of course, my dear mother will....And I know the goodness of God will, and the holy souls themselves will, too!" ...But if his faith and devotion were thus exercised by communing with the members of the Church Suffering, no less scope was afforded by the glorious citizens of the Church Triumphant. He loved and reverenced all the saints, and it was a sweet thought to his enlightened faith, that as a child of God, he could choose as many of them as he desired, and make them *personal friends of his own*: friends to whom he could confide his hopes and fears, and would take a sincere and efficacious interest in his welfare.

Naturally, he felt a special attraction for such saints as had shown a more than ordinary devotion to the Madonna; and therefore, above all others, he cherished a tender devotion to St. Joseph. Of this glorious patriarch he spoke with admiration, exalting his sanctity, greatness and power. He had been particularly impressed by the words of St. Teresa, who affirms in the most positive manner, and in the broadest terms, that she had *never* asked this saint for any grace or favor in vain. Gabriel honored him with touching earnestness, to obtain for himself a holy and happy death: which grace he undoubtedly obtained, as we will see further on. In St. Joseph's honor, he recited daily prayers, consecrated to him the Wednesday of every week, celebrated with extraordinary fervor his three festivals: his espousals, his patronage, and his death; preparing for the last feast, on the seven Sundays preceding the 19th of March, by various exercises. Besides this, he never let a favorable occasion pass by without confessing the feelings of his tender heart for the Foster-Father of Jesus Christ, and the most pure Spouse of the Immaculate Virgin, whom, moreover, he was wont to call by the most endearing names.

Gabriel had also a filial love toward our father and founder, St. Paul of the Cross, who had been raised to the honors of the Beatified by Pius IX, in 1852.

His next patron was St. Francis of Assisi, the Saint of the Crucified, the seraph of love, the herald of evangelical poverty, the chivalrous Knight of Our Lady. It will be remembered that our holy student first saw the light of day in the native city of St. Francis, that he was baptized at the same font in the Cathedral, was known by the same baptismal name: in short the spirit of the patriarch of Assisi seemed to have been imparted to his young namesake, countryman and client. The former, as well as the latter, was carried away by his buoyant nature, and for a time yielded to the attractions of the world; yet both were saved from defilement by their love of Christ's poor, and by their devotion to Christ's mother; they both afterward despised and renounced the world for God's sake, and consecrated all the ardor of their innocent hearts to God alone: *"Deus meus et omnia!"*

Great, too, was Gabriel's devotion toward St. Aloysius, with whom he had in common very many traits of resemblance: and whom he had been first taught to know and love, during his college days in Spoleto, under the zealous Jesuit fathers. A deep religious gratitude made him reverence another Jesuit saint: the blessed martyr Andrew Bobola, to whom he acknowledged the favor of his miraculous cure, when he was hesitating between God and the world, his father's home and the religious cloister.

Another favorite saint of his was Francis de Sales, whose meek and humble spirit he so faithfully copied, and whose works were treasured in the Possenti household. We have already mentioned his regard for St. Alphonsus, whose "Glories of Mary" had been so instrumental in wonderfully increasing his love for *Maria Santissima*.

But for brevity's sake, we must finish this enumeration of Gabriel's saintly favorites. Being far more inclined to mental than vocal prayer, he contented himself with making a litany of his own in honor of all his special patrons, and this he faithfully recited every day. He could truly say "our conversation is in heaven," such being the familiarity and confidence with which he treated his holy patrons, and such his practical understanding of the "communion of saints."

28 His Last Illness

Not many years had elapsed since our Gabriel had been clothed in the religious habit, and from the beginning, his brethren entertained the hope that he would be blessed with a long life, both for the sake of witnessing his marvelous growth in virtue, and that the church might enjoy the advantages of his labors for the good of souls;—but God had disposed otherwise.

Meanwhile, during those short years, his soul had grown ripe for heaven, and it became so pleasing to the Divine Master, that he prepared to take it to Himself. During the last year of Gabriel's life, it was not difficult to foresee that the evening of his earthly career was rapidly coming on. He seemed to have had a secret presentiment of his approaching end, nor did he make any great effort to conceal this feeling: rather, he gave expression to his interior joy at the summons of death. Even had there been no exterior manifestation that the sun of his life was slowly setting, it could not have escaped the vigilant eye of his spiritual director, that another light, the sun of eternal day was fast rising on the horizon of his soul: for more than ever, in that last year, his soul had fallen under the direct influence of the very fountain of light. His interior was illumined no longer by rays, but by streams, or torrents of light, that flooded his mind and consumed his heart more and more: and hence there sprang up in his soul a longing, a thirst for heaven: "As the hart panteth after the fountains of water, so doth my soul desire after Thee, oh my God: when shall I come, and appear before Thy face?" (Psalm 41:2-3) Reflecting too, on the danger of offending God, and growing tepid in the divine service, Gabriel prayed for the grace to die: he even asked for the very malady which eventually carried him off, viz, consumption;[26] and for no other reason, than to be able to make acts of love until he drew his last breath. F. Norbert, hearing of this, and fearing to lose so fervent a disciple, whilst approving of the petition in itself, yet directed him to pray under condition of its being for God's glory, and the greater advantage of his soul. Docile as Gabriel ever was, he at once changed his prayer and did as he was bidden.

For the first four years of his religious life, he had enjoyed, at least apparently, very good health, better indeed than he had had in the world as a secular; for, the regularity of monastic life was well calculated to strengthen his constitution; but during the fifth year, he commenced to feel an ever-increasing weakness which degenerated into unmistakable symptoms of tubercular consumption. Fervent prayers were at once offered by the community, and were requested from outsiders as well. As was said above, Gabriel himself had to join *his* prayers to the heartfelt petitions of his brethren, that he be spared, if it were for the greater glory of God and his own spiritual welfare.

From the first clear symptoms of his fatal malady, he was exempted from the more burdensome exercises of the observance, such as the fasts of rule, and rising at midnight for Matins; but for awhile the fervent youth gently insisted that

---

[26] Editor's Note: A more common word for this disease is Tuberculosis.

His Last Illness

he was well enough to follow the entire observance, for dispensations were to him more onerous than the observance itself.

Despite all the care and attention shown him, his malady went on increasing, until at the end of the year 1861, it broke out into a violent hectic fever, reducing him to a pitiable state of weakness that lasted until the middle of February of the following year, when his hemorrhages began; and then he was in such a state of exhaustion that the physician advised the last sacraments to be given: the poor patient meanwhile remaining perfectly tranquil as though nothing unusual had happened. When he was definitively told that there was real danger of death, and that he should prepare for the reception of the Viaticum, his director knew that he need not take those precautions which are generally resorted to in similar cases, to break the unwelcome tidings gently: he therefore made no mystery about it, but told him plainly that unless a miracle was wrought, he was going to die, and that he should make his last preparations at once. On hearing this, the servant of God, unaware perhaps that he was in such immediate danger, showed for an instant on his face a trace of surprise, but it was followed not merely by resignation but joy: nay, his joy was so pronounced that his director advised him to moderate it.

The community had just finished the chant of the midnight office, and at the signal of the little bell, all repaired to Gabriel's room. He requested to be allowed to rise from his couch and receive the Viaticum on his knees; this being denied, he begged for permission at least to kneel in his bed, but this being also refused, he submitted to the will of his superior. As the Blessed Sacrament was brought into his room, he seemed quite overcome with Christ's grandeur and majesty, supremely penetrated with sentiments of faith and devotion, so that those surrounding his poor bed were affected to tears. Before receiving holy communion, he who had been to all a subject of edification and encouragement in virtue, humbly begged pardon of all for whatever bad example he had ever given: then in tenderness and tears he received his Lord with extraordinary devotion.

Shortly after his communion, F. Norbert being alone with his young disciple, was asked by him to search the papers of the writing table for a small notebook. "I have recorded," said he, "in that little book, all the graces that God has bestowed on me through the hands of the Madonna. I am afraid lest the devil may tempt me to vainglory on account of it. Now, Father, will you take it away, and never show it to anyone?" The director promised. He went even farther, for he said that he would not even look at it himself: then leaving the room, the book was destroyed: a thing for which F. Norbert acknowledged himself very sorry afterward. Well may we all regret this irreparable loss, for that precious little volume was the record of Gabriel's growth in holiness.

The community at Isola feared that Gabriel would die that very night; but he reassured them, saying that his illness would be prolonged for a while; "but," he rejoined, "if the Lord wishes to call me tonight, His will be done!...Whatever happens, may the most holy, most amiable, most adorable will of God be ever done!"

His presentiment was fully realized, for the violence of his fever sensibly abated, and the first sudden outbreak was succeeded by a slow decline which lasted nine days: this was regarded as a disposition of divine Providence to increase his servant's merits, and to give all an opportunity to be further edified by his example. His narrow cell became for his brethren a school, a university of virtue. Whoever entered there, priest, cleric or lay-brother, came forth deeply impressed, often bathed in tears: they would all gladly have remained there indefinitely, without thinking of repose, or anything else.

His patience was admirable and most touching. Though he lay for hours motionless upon his bed of suffering, without being able to change his position, on account of his extreme prostration, he never uttered a syllable of complaint, but encouraged himself to bear with the inconveniences of his sickness, by recalling to mind the agonies of Jesus on the cross, and the sorrows of the mother standing beneath it. When asked occasionally what pain he felt, he would mention no other than the weakness and weariness resulting from his monotony of posture; yet as a matter of fact, he had a very high fever which often made his mind wander, and then he would unconsciously show how great his sufferings really were, by the writhing of his body, and the groans that were wrung from him in these paroxysms of pain. But he watched most carefully lest he should betray how much he suffered, as long as he was fully master of himself: he refrained even from moaning, no matter at what cost to himself, in order to spare the feelings of those around him, and not to disturb them, however slightly.

Nor was he satisfied with practicing patience: in spite of his condition, he found means to exercise himself in mortification as well. He took with the greatest avidity the most disagreeable medicines, but he swallowed them with deliberate slowness in order to mortify his palate, and he cheerfully submitted to many things entailing physical pain, when ordered by the infirmarian, or the attending physician, even when he knew full well that they would be of no use whatever. "Yet," writes his director, "when I happened to be alone with him, he would complain to me of being so immortified, of not having the courage to suffer, and of being wanting in virtue. I strove to comfort him by bidding him be satisfied with offering up to God what ever he might have to suffer: and I ordered him not to hesitate to tell those in the room, whenever he stood in need of anything: that in this manner, he could practice both obedience and mortification of will, and his companions exercise fraternal charity."

More striking however than his patience or his mortification, was his cheerfulness. To judge from his look of peacefulness, one might have concluded that the dear youth was in perfect health, and his manner was always gracious, almost mirthful. When his visitors would ask with evident concern and gravity how he was feeling, he would smilingly answer: "Just about the same, like the blind beggar's story!"...And this light-heartedness proceeded not only from his own interior peace, but from his exquisite charity which made him shrink from being in any way burdensome to others.

We need not wonder then, that Gabriel's fellow-students vied with each other in charitable eagerness to assist their sick brother, both by night and day. "They would come," says F. Norbert, "to ask me to appoint them to do something or other for him. One would complain that I did not allow him to go to the sick room in his regular turn; another, that he was sent away much too soon, in fact before his regular time was fully out!...Every one would have preferred to remain, were it in their power."

One of his companions asked Gabriel to recommend him to the Madonna, for a very special intention. Now, this religious had great confidence in his brother's intercession, and what he wanted was to be cured of an ailment that was giving him a deal of trouble. Gabriel replied simply: "Oh, yes, Confrater, I'll do that." After a little while, however, when nobody thought anything further about what had passed between them, suddenly the servant of God turned to his companion, and said: "My dear Confrater, the favor you ask for is not according to God's will, you know: it is a cross that you will have to carry until death." On hearing this, the religious was, as it were, stunned for a while, regarding the whole thing as plainly supernatural, since he gave Gabriel no inkling whatsoever of what his intention was; but coming to himself, he said: "Well, may God's will be done!"—As a matter of fact, the prediction was verified: the ailment[27] continued to trouble him all his life long, but encouraging himself by remembering his saintly brother's words, he submitted with perfect resignation, commending himself anew to Gabriel's prayers, after the latter had exchanged this world for a throne of glory in heaven.

When the time came for administering the sacrament of Extreme Unction, Gabriel asked that its effects be once more brought to his mind, and with fervent sentiments of faith and contrition, he disposed himself to receive it. As the fever had impaired his hearing, he begged the officiating priest to read the prayers in a rather loud tone of voice, so that he might understand everything, and accompany the sacred rite with intelligent devotion.

"During the whole course of this illness," says his director, "he only continued (but with even greater heartiness) what he had been doing all through his life; that is, uniting his soul with God, making frequent aspirations now to Jesus in the Blessed Sacrament, now to Jesus Crucified, as well as to the Mother of dolors. He used to hold his profession-cross in his hand, or he asked to have it placed before his eyes: the same he did with his little picture of the *Addolorata*: and upon these two objects of his heart's love, he frequently pressed his burning lips." During his life he used to make his ejaculations interiorly, or at most in an undertone, so as not to attract the attention of others; but during the time of his sickness he uttered them aloud; he even made them in such a strong voice

---

[27] Editor's Note: The ailment was a painful hernia.

that his director had often to chide him for it; but the progress of the malady made him forget the recommendation.

The hour fixed by God's holy will for Gabriel's departure from this world, was now rapidly approaching. His bodily frame, consumed by an unconquerable fever, was nearing its dissolution; but the spirit within, more vigorous than ever before, seemed to thrill with joy at the prospect of deliverance. No more fitting time could have been chosen for a Passionist to die, for just then the community was celebrating the octave of the solemn commemoration of the Passion of Jesus Christ.

29 His Holy Death

It was the night of the 26th of February, and as the symptoms became more serious, Gabriel's fellow-students did not leave his bedside even for a moment, but his director, perceiving no immediate danger of death, decided to rest a while, for he was exhausted with fatigue and loss of sleep. Still try as he would, he could not fall asleep: a persistent feeling told him that he was deserting his post of duty. As to him alone were known the secrets of Gabriel's conscience, who else could comfort him in case of need? No longer hesitating, F. Norbert returned to the sick-room, determined to watch over his dying child to the last. He soon found out that he had been guided by the mysterious Providence of God, for, as he was sitting in a corner of the room, suddenly he heard Confrater Gabriel say in a loud voice, and with much feeling: "*Vulnera tua, merita mea*: Thy wounds, O Lord, are my merits!" "At first," the director tells us, "I did not take great account of this, because the patient often recited little prayers in a similar tone of voice. But soon, he repeated a second and a third time, the same words, in a louder and stronger voice. At once suspecting the cause, and drawing near, I asked him confidentially: 'Are you tempted?' 'Yes, father, I am,' he replied, quite dejectedly....'Is it presumption, or despair?' I then asked. 'Presumption.' I then helped him by suggesting sentiments suited to his needs, and sprinkled the room with holy water: whereupon he became calm;" but the prudent director continued watching and praying.

Meanwhile, the violence of the fever brought on occasional wanderings of mind: but they were of such a nature as not completely to destroy consciousness; so that recovering himself quickly, Gabriel laughed softly to himself, saying: "I was really wandering then, wasn't I?"—still, even in his delirium, he was always speaking of holy things.

Suddenly, the dying youth frowns: he becomes greatly troubled: and tightly shutting his eyes, he looks with disgust in another direction. This was his second struggle: this time against the vile demon of impurity. F. Norbert asks what is troubling him? Gabriel, half angry and wholly surprised, answers: "How do women enter here? They mustn't be here; who let them in? O Mary, my mother, chase them away, make them go!" The director at once sprinkled the room with holy water, which scattered for the nonce the foul spirits of hell: and the patient regained his wonted peace. But it did not last long. The devil hoping to profit by the weakness of a dying man, returns cowardly to the assault, reproducing upon Gabriel's imagination the same indecent images. This was his third and last combat. No sooner was he aware of the nearness of danger, than he showed his aversion to it. "How could that lady get in here?" he cried. "They are not allowed here. Why did you let her in? Chase her out, right away! O, my mother, my Lady, drive her away!"—And in saying these words, he showed such a loathing for those indecent suggestions, and did such violence to himself, and resisted with such heartiness, that the bystanders knew not what to admire most, the firmness of his courage, or his purity of heart.

Thrice had he been exposed to great danger, thrice did his cruel enemies close in around his poor dying soul, but trusting in his Mother's help, and with her name upon his parched lips, he completely routed the fiends of hell, and passed unscathed through the ordeal. To spare themselves further defeat, they troubled him no more; and Gabriel enjoyed thenceforward an unbroken peace. The remaining hours of the night until daybreak, he employed in his wonted fervent aspirations to Jesus Crucified, to his Blessed Mother, and to the dear St. Joseph. His eyes were fixed either on his crucifix or the picture of the *Addolorata*, but these exercises were interspersed with many little acts of kindness and gratitude, in favor of those who waited on him.

As the sun was rising on the morning of the twenty-seventh of February, Gabriel unexpectedly turned to his spiritual director who was sitting at his bedside, and joyfully said to him: "Father, you might give me absolution, now." As there was, however, no change for the worse in Gabriel's condition, the director did not think fit to accede to the request, but simply replied: "My son, it isn't time yet: but I'll attend to it myself, when the time does come." Gabriel made no reply. He seemed notwithstanding, to be well aware of the nearness of death; that in fact, he had only a few minutes more to live. So then, after a very short interval, he turned to F. Norbert, and said: "I have just made my act of contrition: Father, do give me absolution," at the same time uncovering his head and joining his hands. This time F. Norbert absolved him, and promised that he would renew the absolution later on, especially when he was actually dying. Gabriel then asked for his little picture of Our Lady of Sorrows. An old print from his breviary, all soiled from daily use, representing Jesus Crucified and the Queen of Martyrs, was given him. Taking it eagerly in both hands, he pressed it to his lips, bathed it with his tears, and covered it with kisses. Then addressing Jesus and Mary in terms of the tenderest love, he pressed the picture to his heart, as though he wished to stamp it there indelibly. All in the room were filled with sentiments of reverential awe. From time to time, his spiritual Father suggested some pious thoughts, less indeed to enkindle in him the love of God and Our Lady, than to make it burn with a still brighter glow. Uncovering his breast, Gabriel put the image of those he loved so well over his heart; then crossing his hands, he embraced the picture with such earnestness, such loving fervor, such tenderness, that no one could have remained unmoved; for one could see in the dying youth, that his saintly soul was reflected in his radiant face. When he had thus put the image of Jesus Crucified and the Sorrowful Virgin upon his heart, he raised his eyes to heaven with a look of eager and joyful expectancy, and cried out in an animated voice, but with confidence and love indescribable: "O my Mother, make haste!" Afterward, he recited calmly the following prayer separating and emphasizing his words:

"*Maria, Mater gratiae,*	"*Mother of Grace, O Mary blest,*
Mater misericordiae,	*Sweet mercy's fount, to thee we fly,*
Tu nos ab hoste protege,	*Shield us from harm, and take us hence*
Et mortis hora suscipe."	*To thy dear bosom, when we die.*"

With the same profound feeling, he recited the well-known prayers:

"Jesus, Mary and Joseph, I give you my heart and my soul.

"Jesus, Mary and Joseph, assist me in my last agony.

"Jesus, Mary and Joseph, may I breathe forth my soul in peace with you."

When he had finished those ejaculations, he composed himself once more, his eyes closed, his hands tightly clasped over the picture pressed to his heart. Then we noticed that he was just about to die, for his breathing became very perceptibly slower. The lector had the signal for the community rung at once, and all who were not then engaged in celebrating or serving Mass, immediately repaired to the sick-room, to assist their dying brother by their united prayers. There was no agony, not even a trace of pain on his quiet face; he was like one about to fall asleep. All at once, his face lights up with happiness and devotion, and opening his eyes with a lively transport of joy, he gazes fixedly in midair toward the left side. He appears as if face to face with some magnificent sight, overpowered by an awe-inspiring majesty, for which he lovingly, longingly sighs, and thus, without the least bodily movement, he ceases to breathe and joyfully passes out of this life like one softly falling asleep. His hands were folded over the picture of Jesus Crucified and the Mother of Sorrows, his face was wreathed in smiles, and his eyes still seeming to drink in that marvelous vision. During his holy life Gabriel had often expressed his belief that his gracious Mother and Queen would surely come to take his soul with her to heaven, and it

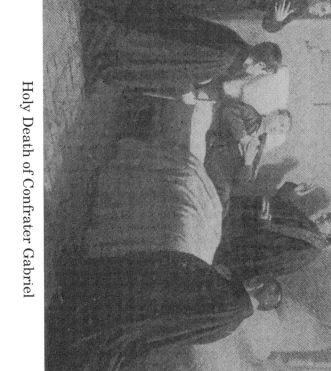

Holy Death of Confrater Gabriel

seems that his hope was not confounded. "Consumed by the ardor of divine love, rather than by the violence of disease, comforted and rapt in an ecstasy by the apparition of his heavenly Mother (whom he loved with an immeasurable affection) he was sweetly received by her; and laden with merits, left for heaven." (Such is the judgment of several princes of the Church, as well as of his own spiritual director.)[28]

All the religious were deeply moved, many weeping through devotion. One of them would not believe that Gabriel was dead; another struck his breast, saying: "So many years am I in the service of God, and yet so backward; while he in so short a time became a saint, and has had such a beautiful death!" Others too, gave vent to their emotion in diverse ways.

Gabriel Possenti, of Our Lady of Sorrows, died on Thursday, February 27th, 1862, in our retreat of the Immaculate Virgin at Isola di Gran Sasso, Province of Abruzzo, Italy, in the twenty-fourth year of his age, having lived in the congregation of the Passion a little over five years and seven months.

After his death, the body was clothed in the holy habit, his profession-cross was put into his hands (which were joined over his breast), he was then laid upon a bare board in that same poor cell where he breathed his last, his head sprinkled with ashes and resting on a few bricks. All this was done in accordance with the prescription of our rule. Toward evening he was carried into the church, where on the following morning his solemn obsequies took place; he was then privately buried

---

[28] Cardinals Parocchi, Di Pietro and Manara.

in the vault reserved for the religious of the community, near the door of the church.

30 His Growing Fame

No persons are less credulous, no persons exact more convincing proofs before recognizing superior holiness, than those who make profession of tending toward perfection. Yes, if there be a place where it is really difficult to be rated as a saint, that place is the monastery, or the convent. And yet, such was the eminence of sanctity evidenced in Confrater Gabriel's life, that although his love of humility made him seek to be unknown, he was unanimously acknowledged as a saint, proposed to all as an exemplar, while all were struck with admiration at his faultless conduct. His blessed death did but increase his fame. "The reputation of the servant of God," says F. Norbert, "did not cease after his burial: rather, all who had known him personally, still treasure his memory as of a great servant of God. Coupled with this reputation, was the confidence that he inspired in his power with the Most High," for not a few obtained special and extraordinary favors through his mediation.

But alas! the revolutionary storm which had broken out in Italy since 1859, and in the midst of which Gabriel had expired, was raging still. Far from abating its fury, it had but increased as the years rolled by. Lombardy, Tuscany, Parma, the Marches and the Romagna had successively become the prey of the masonic sects, that governed "United Italy" in the name of Victor Emmanuel. The usurpers made haste to abolish every law and institution distinctively Catholic: by the right of might, all ecclesiastical property passed into the hands of the state. As ever, the valiant sons of Loyola were the first victims of the injustice and fury of the revolution. They were driven from their peaceful homes; and in their wake, soon followed the other religious orders, both of men and women, in the Pontifical domain: henceforth their right to live, and their right to the pursuit of happiness, were shamefully, unjustly and inconsistently denied in a land, the air of which was then ringing with the cry of "Liberty." The Passionist monasteries had little to excite the greed and envy of the mighty, but they could not be tolerated: so the poor retreat, lost in the solitude of Isola, did not escape: a few religious watching and praying were too great a menace to the stability of the new kingdom of "redeemed Italy." The little community was dispersed in 1863: the church and monastery remained untenanted: the sacramental lamp was quenched before the empty tabernacle, and the sacred remains of the young and saintly Passionist religious were left to the care of the protecting angels.

It would have been no wonder if in the midst of such unfavorable circumstances, the memory of the servant of God were forgotten little by little: but the contrary is precisely what came to pass. In the nature of things, the life of a Passionist student is so hidden in the solitude of the retreat, that he is almost completely unknown to the outside world. Even in the retreat itself, his familiar intercourse is limited to his director, lector and a few companions. Yet, after the lapse of many years, Gabriel's memory had not died out among the simple people of Isola, in whose midst he had lived only for a short time comparatively, and whose knowledge of him was gathered from seeing him about the church on feast-days, or from meeting him with his fellow-students on their customary walks through the country.

It was however in the bosom of the congregation, of which he had been such an edifying member, that his name was cherished with ever-increasing confidence and admiration. The testimony of F. Francis Xavier, then general of the order, will stand for all others; and we have already seen in an earlier chapter, how little inclined he was to exaggeration. "I entertain," he says in his deposition, "a special devotion toward the servant of God, because I remember with admiration his many virtues: and often too, do I recommend myself to his intercession, for I have always looked upon him as a saint. After his death, his reputation for sanctity not only remained undiminished, but it has been increasing and spreading, both among our own religious, as well as among outsiders." As time went on, there grew in the hearts of all a desire to see our beloved brother raised to the honors of the altar; and thus it came to pass in 1891, that the superiors of the congregation after mature deliberation, resolved that the necessary steps be taken for his beatification and canonization. Toward the autumn of 1892, a delegation representing the Bishop of Penne, (in whose diocese Isola di Gran Sasso is situated), was sent privately to examine Gabriel's place of burial and the condition of his remains. But on arriving at the poor deserted church, the commissioners found that some hundreds of persons from the surrounding district had already gathered there, determined to resist with all their strength any attempt to remove the relics of the servant of God. Who had told them of a project, every step of which was conducted with prudent secrecy? But the attendance of the people was vastly greater on the morrow the 18th of October, when the delegates of the episcopal *curia* set out to make the formal recognition and authentication of the remains of the servant of God, and prepare them for removal to another retreat. The postulator of the cause, F. Germanus, gives us a graphic recital of what then transpired. The day and hour had been kept a secret, nor did anyone outside of the commission know what was going to be done. Yet no sooner had the committee started from the town of Isola, and commenced the journey to the desolate church of the Passionists, than a strange sight obtruded itself upon their notice. All the paths leading to the old monastery were covered with people. Although it was a weekday, and the busiest part of the vintage,[29] from all the surrounding villages the people flocked to the church, singing devout hymns as they hastened on their way. When the delegates reached the hill, they found it covered with about four thousand people, men and women, old and young, all attired in their gayest, as if they had been urgently entreated to attend some solemn ceremonial. What brought them there? Comparatively few had known Confrater Gabriel personally, (for it was now thirty years after his holy death,) and perhaps the majority of those

---

[29] Editor's Note: This means it was the busiest time of year for harvesting grapes grown for winemaking.

who were there present had but seldom if ever heard even of his name. Who can explain it, save by an instinct of divine Providence, that secretly and suddenly moved the hearts of those simple Christian folk? How explain their reluctance, nay their positive unwillingness to allow the mortal remains of God's faithful servant to be removed?

The church was packed with people, and they obstinately refused to leave the sacred precincts. "We have come here to see to our own affair," said they, "and we will not depart, till we make sure that no one will take away from us the relics of *'the holy religious'!*"

The delegates, therefore, made up their minds to leave the remains where they were, and had perforce to be satisfied with authenticating them, and placing them in a more suitable tomb. In order to empty the church, so as to allow the necessary formalities to be carried out according to law, the following expedient was resorted to. A few of the principal inhabitants of each village were chosen to represent the rest, and thus, before a gathering of two or three hundred persons, the canonical requirements began. On entering the burial-vault, nothing but the bones of Confrater Gabriel were found, the flesh having been entirely consumed: even of the clothes, nothing remained but the leathern girdle and the "sign" which is worn over the heart. Two experienced physicians arranged the bones in their natural position, on a white linen cloth; then they were enclosed in a double casket, which was sealed with the episcopal seal. After this, the church-doors were opened, and the crowd which had patiently waited for several hours surged round the casket, covering it with kisses and tears: some put wreaths and flowers upon Gabriel's coffin, and preserved them afterward as precious souvenirs. "Verily, God had spoken to the hearts of His people," writes F. Germanus, "and it was He who had moved them to such singular piety and devotion." Not less marvelous was the orderliness of such a large crowd, for though densely packed in a small church, though the enthusiasm of their religious sentiments ran high, there was neither noise nor any unseemly behavior: not a word or action unbecoming a place of divine worship.

On the following day, October 18th, in the presence of the same faithful people, the casket was carried to the chapel of St. Paul of the Cross, and was laid in a specially prepared sepulchre on the epistle side. Shortly afterward a mortuary slab was erected with the following inscription:

CORPUS SERVI DEI GABRIELIS A VIRGINE DOLOROSA CONGREGATIONIS PASSIONIS D. N. J. C., CLERICI PROFESSI HEIC DEPOSITUM XV KAL. NOV. MDCCCXCII. ANNIS AB OBITU XXX.	The body of the servant of God, Gabriel of our Lady of Sorrows, Professed Cleric of the Congregation of the Passion of Jesus Christ, was deposited in this place, October 18th, 1892, thirty years after his death.

New Tomb of Blessed Gabriel

31 Our Latest Wonder-Worker

The 17th of October, when the official recognition of the remains of the servant of God took place, was an ideal autumn day amid the Abruzzi hills. The Italian blue of the sky was like the mantle of the Madonna stretched in its undescribable beauty: not a breeze to carry far and near the perfume of the vineyards: when, toward noon, whilst the sacred ceremonies were going on in the church, and precisely at the very moment when the relics of the servant of God were being extracted from their first resting-place, a tiny cloud coming from the summit of the Gran Sasso swiftly moved toward the church, then stopping and spreading, it inundated the sacred precincts with a flood of rain, while not a drop fell outside of the monastery grounds. —A presage this from heaven, that the bones of Confrater Gabriel would be a source of blessing and graces, in favor of mankind. Such an inference is plainly warranted by the authentic list of cures, which from that very day have made Isola one of the most frequented of modern shrines, and has elevated our dear Gabriel to the dignity of being popularly considered "the modern Thaumaturgus."[30]

---

[30] Editor's Note: Translated into English, the word means Wonder-Worker, a title used of saints who work tremendous miracles. St. Gabriel is exceptional with respect to this title, for it is typically applied to saints who perform miracles during their earthly pilgrimage. As a testimony to the saint's popularity, another biography of St. Gabriel, written in the 1960s, claims "on good authority" that the only two shrines that receive more pilgrims each year than the shrine at Isola are Lourdes and Fátima. (Happy Was My Youth by Edmund Burke, C. P., Page 160)

"It is not our intention to forestall the solemn judgment of the church, to whom alone it belongs to pronounce sentence in matters concerning the supernatural order: we will only narrate as human, historical facts, what has been seen with the eyes, and as it were, touched with the hands, in many parts of Italy, and even in distant lands, for the past four years. While kneeling at Gabriel's tomb, or by using his relics, even by devoutly applying the dust gathered from his grave, the blind see, the dumb speak, the deaf hear, the cripples, the paralytics, and those afflicted with the most serious maladies, (some of whom were on their deathbed,) have instantaneously recovered their health, by invoking his name." Thus wrote F. Germanus in 1896. Up to that time, three hundred and eighty prodigies were recorded, but God alone knows the exact number of favors conferred, for many good people content themselves with offering thanks at Gabriel's tomb, and depart rejoicing on their way, without making themselves known.

For the honor of God and His chosen servant, we will now narrate a few well authenticated cases from the official documents, premising that the first two were accepted for his beatification as undoubted miracles, after the most rigid scrutiny.

No. 1. Mary Mazzarella, aged twenty, lived with her parents in the village of Isola. For nearly three years she had been suffering with serious complications affecting her lungs, stomach and spine, with constant daily fever and headache. At first there seemed to be question only of gastralgia, or neuralgia of the stomach, but clear symptoms soon made it evident that acute tubercular phthisis or consumption had set in. Three hemorrhages ensued. Gradually losing all appetite, the physician allowed her to take anything she might fancy, but her daily food hardly amounted to two or three spoonfuls of the pottage prepared for the family. Her condition steadily became worse. In January, 1892, she experienced great pains all through her body, and six ulcerous wounds broke out. These wounds went on enlarging, and prevented her from resting either by day or night. From five of the wounds putrid matter was discharged. She became so weak that she could not stand on her feet, and was unable to bear the light. The summer heat inconvenienced her greatly, so that she could hardly breathe; then, loss of sleep joined with the constant oppression on her chest so affected her voice, that she could speak only with difficulty. The remedies that were prescribed were of no avail, and she lost all confidence in medicine. In August she was persuaded to allow Dr. Tattoni to attend her. After a careful examination, he declared the case hopeless. Finally she turned to heaven for her cure, and with all the confidence and tenderness of a loving child, besought her Blessed Mother to help her. Now it happened that one day in October, having fallen asleep, she saw a beautiful lady with a child in her arms, and was told to go and pray at the tomb of the holy young Passionist at the monastery, and use some of his relics, assuring her that she would be cured. At the request of her uncle, F. Germanus went to see her.

This is what he says: "When first I saw her, I was seized with horror. She seemed to me like a corpse, the only sign of life being a slow and painful breathing. Propped up with pillows, she was lying motionless, tormented with six large, purulent ulcers that gave her no rest either by day or night. It was then three months since she had taken food, and I remember saying on that occasion that, if the Blessed Virgin cured her, it would be a miracle like the resurrection of Lazarus." This visit took place two days after the ceremonies described in the preceding chapter. F. Germanus did not give credence to the story of her vision, saying that we ought not to tempt God; nor should the patient be put to the discomfort of being brought up to the church; in fact, he said that such a journey might even hasten her death, and that if the Blessed Virgin was willing to obtain for her the grace of being cured, she would do it without the journey at all. "F. Germanus came to see me on October 20th," the girl herself informs us. "He hung about my neck a crucifix belonging to Confrater Gabriel, the servant of God, and he put on me also the leathern girdle which was taken out of his grave. The Passionist father greatly comforted me, exhorting me to have confidence in the intercession of this holy religious. He told me to make a vow to go barefoot to the monastery church, in case the favor would be granted, assuring me that after three days of prayer made with my heart rather than my lips, I would obtain my cure.

"Meanwhile the malady did not abate, but I recommended myself the best I could to Confrater Gabriel. The triduum was to finish on Sunday, October 23rd. Saturday evening I felt very, very sick, and my people at home were more than usually downcast, for when they carried me to my room, they had great trouble in undressing me, and getting me ready for bed."

So far poor Mary's account. We learn from other sources, that their anxiety was even greater that night than she imagined. Her mother, who had no longer any hope of her daughter's cure, as a result of the triduum, and fearing besides that the girdle might inconvenience her, was about to take it away from her child; but Mary objected, remarking that the whole night was still wanting to complete the prescribed three days.

"Toward the first dawn of the following day, Sunday," (to resume Mary's own narrative) "I told my sister to recite the litany, and to join me in praying to the servant of God. While I was saying the litany, there came upon me a quiet sleep, such as I had not had for a long time. After awhile I awoke full of joy, feeling that I was cured,—completely cured. My strength had returned, the sores had closed, and one of them (which was very large and was about to open) disappeared altogether. Filled with delight I said to my sister, 'Get up! I am cured! Confrater Gabriel has done the miracle for me!' For well-nigh eight months I had been unable to wait upon myself: my people had to assist me in everything. Now, that morning, I got up at once, dressed myself in haste, and went down to the kitchen. My sister would not believe her eyes: she kept by my side, afraid lest it all might be a delusion, somehow or other. But I went down-stairs and stood before my parents and the servant-maid, who were all in the kitchen. My mother was astounded when she saw me, but I said to her: 'Mamma, don't be afraid: Confrater Gabriel has performed the miracle for me,' and to reassure my poor mother all the more, I took the baby from her arms into mine."

Now it happened that the feast-day of Isola was celebrated on that Sunday, and there was in the village an extraordinary concourse of strangers. Mary's father, beside himself with emotion, ran out of the house, weeping. The neighbors crowded around, thinking that his daughter had just died; and lo! there was Mary among them, sound and happy: all were deeply moved, and wept for joy. That same morning, Mary went to the parish church with her parents, heard Mass and received holy Communion. The next day she went to the sanctuary of Our Lady of Favors outside of the village; and on the following Tuesday, that is on October 25th, two days after her cure, together with all her family, all barefoot like herself, and accompanied by the whole population of Isola, she went to fulfill her vow at the tomb of God's servant. She walked all the way, going and returning, a distance of about five miles, and has enjoyed perfect health ever since. This cure has been attested by the sworn statements of Mary herself, her parents, Father Ciaverelli, and the two physicians, Dr. Tauri, and Dr. Rossi, and several others.

By the cure of this young woman, the Christian public came to know that it would not be deceived in placing its trust in such a powerful servant of God. Thereupon, everybody implored his intercession, and asked for all kinds of favors, with the most ardent faith. In a biography of our dear Gabriel, published only six months after this first miracle, Monsignor Jezzoni could say: "There is scarcely anyone in all this country side sick or afflicted, spiritually or temporally needy, who fails to turn to this young servant of God. From villages, towns and cities, far and near, the unfortunate and the stricken come, or are carried to the little Passionist church at Isola, as to one of the most renowned sanctuaries; and ever so many return to their homes consoled and cured."

No. 2. For more than twelve years, a peasant named Dominic Tiberi, of Colliberti, a village near Isola, suffered from rupture. Through carelessness, and the circumstances of his life as a farmer, his condition grew steadily worse; and at last, his very life became insupportable, so many and so grievous were his pains and inconveniences. "He was horribly ruptured," said his neighbors, and as his deformity was very evident to all, it inspired terror rather than pity, and to add to the chalice of his bitterness, he was often made game of in the public streets.

One day when his pain had become so agonizing that he thought he was at the point of death, he dragged himself somehow to Bl. Gabriel's tomb. He knelt with the rest as they prayed, each one for himself, and he asked with lively faith just for a little relief. Then bending down he touched with his hand the marble gravestone, and forthwith passed that hand over his rupture. At that very instant all his pains stopped, the rupture completely vanished, and Dominic was able to return to his house without the slightest fatigue, climbing with alacrity the rough, steep pathway of the hill on which he lived.

In relating the above miracle, F. Germanus, C.P., the Postulator of the Cause, says: "Having met Mr. Tiberi in the town of Isola, I brought him at once to the druggist's where he had often been treated when his rupture was at its worst. I summoned a doctor to examine him; three other physicians examined him afterward; and all four declared that there was no trace of any kind of rupture. In fact, one of these doctors, who bragged of his religious infidelity, claimed that Mr. Tiberi's condition was so perfectly normal as to make him think that there never was a rupture there at all!"

No. 3. Titus Ortensi, a gentleman living in Castiglione, suffered from the same ailment for several years. The doctors who had charge of him, as well as his intimate friends and acquaintances unanimously testified that his condition was most pitiable. The poor man himself, already advanced in years, had as much as he could do to move about in his own house. It sometimes happens in periods of great sickness or other danger, that even the least devout turn to God in prayer and hope; so, Mr. Ortensi, eager to be cured, went at night, at the cost of indescribable pain and inconvenience, to our little church at Isola, some five or six times altogether. Although at that hour he found the door locked, he knelt down as best he might, praying with great earnestness, and confident as to the result. The last time, his prayer was unusually fervent: God heard it, and Titus returned home sound and well. The doctors of course examined him, and great was their surprise on finding no trace whatever of his former malady. He enjoyed the best of health for many years, and often detailed to interested enquirers, with tears of gratitude in his eyes, both the misery which he had endured for so long, and the completeness of his cure. The monastery church and Bl. Gabriel's tomb were his delight; thither he very frequently repaired, and in spite of his having to walk several miles to get there, he was one of the very first of the crowd that daily gathered in that favored sanctuary, either to solicit special graces, or to thank heaven for having received them.

It would seem that our Gabriel has been made in these latter days the particular patron of those afflicted with rupture.[31] As a matter of fact, the number of those who have been cured of it through his intercession must be counted by hundreds: men and women, the aged and even little children. Their unfortunate malady disappeared in an instant, together with all its consequences; some by simply invoking the servant of God and asking his help; others by making on their rupture the sign of the cross with the hand that touched his tomb; but generally the cure was effected by applying some of the dust from his grave.

No. 4. Sister Mary of Pompeii, belonging to the convent of Reparation in Rome, fell grievously sick in May, 1890, with acute cerebro-spinal anemia, which was aggravated by an obstinate pleuro-pneumonia, and a tumor of the size of an orange on her right side, with concomitant menorrhagia. This formidable combination brought her to death's door, and the last sacraments were administered. The poor Sister lay like one already dead, motionless and colorless, bereft of the power of either speaking or hearing; confused in mind, oppressed

---

[31] Editor's Note: The more common term for the ailment is a hernia.

with inflammation of the brain and by convulsions that weakened her more and more; and finally she was harassed by bronchial troubles that made paralysis of the lungs imminent. Her cough, her prostration and her difficulty of breathing were extreme, and at last, every kind of medicine was discontinued, for they but aggravated her sufferings, and rendered the taking of food more difficult, and sometimes even impossible.

At this juncture, Sr. Mary and her companions in religion had recourse to God, to obtain her cure from Him, if such were His holy will. Somebody suggested that they should solicit the intercession of Confrater Gabriel of Our Lady of Sorrows, whereupon the sick Sister with all the community commenced a novena. When it was ended, Sr. Mary was suffering more than usual, and her condition became worse in many ways. The following afternoon, when the M. Superior visited her according to custom, she said to her: "My daughter, if you had faith in the servant of God, you'd get up and go around." At these words of the superior, the invalid felt a strange movement within herself, as if her bodily strength had suddenly returned and she answered: "Well, then, Mother, give me my clothes!" Before giving them to her, the prayers of the novena were once more recited, and then Sr. Mary dressed herself without any assistance, and found herself instantly cured, so that she was able to follow all the exercises of the community that same day.

The physician who had charge of this wonderful case has freely and fully admitted all this under oath, and his deposition is part of the Apostolic Process for Gabriel's beatification, this being one of the three miracles submitted to the S. Congregation of Rites, and accepted after the most searching scrutiny.

A few further details are given by the Postulator of the Cause. Sr. Mary's cure was instantaneous and complete, so that there was no trace left of all her various ailments. What is more striking still, her extreme emaciation, the natural result of so long a period of sickness and prostration, likewise disappeared, and was replaced by the plumpness, color and freshness of young and healthy womanhood.

No. 5. Philomena Pinciotti of Castel Castagna, a girl of ten years, was afflicted with a cystic tumor of a cancerous nature, which for five years had been steadily growing from about the size of an egg, when it was first noticed, until it became quite evident to the sight, and was as hard as a stone. It resisted all treatment. There's no telling how much the little one suffered, as the swelling, encroaching more and more upon the internal organs, hindered the taking and the assimilation of food, while the constant pain it caused, deprived her of sleep. Thus she was wasting slowly away, moving to compassion all who saw her. One fine day her mother led her to Isola with great difficulty, and they prayed together before Gabriel's tomb; after which they procured a little dust from his grave, and having applied it to the affected part, they started back to their native village. Whilst on the way, the artless child asked her mother to stop for a minute that she might tie the waist of her dress, which had become very loose. But the mother paid no attention to her. However, when they reached home, the tumor had vanished, all pain had ceased, and the girl's health and color were perfectly restored.

No. 6. In consequence of a serious attack of typhoid fever, Egidius Guagnozzi of Castiglione della Valle, aged sixty-two, was utterly deaf, so that he could not even hear the ringing of the church bells. Medical authorities teach that when deafness results from such diseases, it is of a very serious nature, and can hardly ever be cured.

Poor Egidius was given up by the doctors, and had no hope himself of being cured, when suddenly the thought came to him of praying to the servant of God. He went to the monastery church, prayed at Gabriel's tomb, put some of the miraculous dust in his ears, and instantly recovered his hearing perfectly.

No. 7. Blindness cured.—Rose Corini, aged forty, of Nereto, without any previous sickness, suddenly lost the sight of both eyes, by amaurosis, or paralysis of the optic nerves. With her eyes wide open, she could fix them upon the sun without the least impression being made upon them. The local physicians after treating her in vain, remanded her to the clinical institute of Bologna, there to undergo a surgical operation. She however paid little heed to the recommendation, and continued to lament her misfortune.

Being in this condition of mind, the servant of God (whom she had never seen before), appeared to her in a dream, and invited her to pay him a visit in the monastery church at Isola. When she awoke, she at once resolved to go, and set out with her husband, being encouraged by the doctors to make the pilgrimage. When near the hill on which the church stands, she heard a number of voices singing pious hymns, (it was a procession on its way to the church,) whereupon the poor woman said in a spirit of faith: "Well, I am blind now, but on my return, I will be able to see." She was led by the hand to the church, and when she arrived at the tomb, she knelt down praying with copious tears. Then having touched the tomb with a handkerchief she applied it to her face, merely asking to be able to see with one eye. The church was filled with people devoutly engaged in prayer: all at once, the silence was broken with cries of joy: for at that moment Rose had opened her left eye, and was able to see perfectly, and the very first thing she saw was Gabriel's picture on the monument. She at once recognized in him the young religious, who had appeared to her at home.

Now, there was an innkeeper at Montorio, in whose house Rose and her husband had stopped on their way to Isola. This incredulous man had remarked that he would indeed believe in the miracles, which were attributed to Gabriel's intercession, if this woman returned healed. Great then was his surprise when his guest came back cured on the following evening.

A first favor emboldens one to ask for another. Rose began, soon after her return, to pray for the recovery of her right eye also. She applied to it one of Gabriel's relics, and by the mercy of God, her petition was granted.

No. 8. Lucy Callisti was suffering from keratitis or inflammation of the cornea of the right eye; but while under the treatment of Dr. Petrilli, an experienced surgeon, the ailment extended also to her left eye, thus completely depriving her of sight. Her friends and neighbors, touched by such a misfortune in a girl of sixteen, suggested to her mother that Lucy should have recourse to the intercession of Confrater Gabriel. The maiden was brought twice to the tomb of the servant of God, and after the second time, she went home completely cured.

The attending physician states that this disease is of so serious a character, that even supposing the possibility of a perfect cure, this could not occur except gradually, and after a long time.

No. 9. Anthony Egidius of Capsano, a child nine years old, became blind in both eyes as the sequel of a disease with which he had been afflicted. Remedies were quite useless: he grew worse and worse, while his spasms of pain were indescribable. Feeling herself inspired to ask from heaven a cure that human aid could not confer, his mother led little Anthony to the grave of Bl. Gabriel. Whilst she prayed with tears and sobs, her son stretched himself on the flat marble slab of the tomb, and fell fast asleep. After his little nap, he got up, and was able to see everything clearly; the film which had entirely covered the iris and pupil of both eyes had fallen away, the inflammation and agonizing pain had subsided forever; for since that hour, he was completely freed from his ailment.

No. 10. Mary Ann Conti was blind in both eyes. The doctors held out a hope of cure if she submitted to an operation; but her courage failed her, and she turned instead to

Bl. Gabriel, and with ardent faith asked him to help her. She then went to pray at his tomb, and returned home cured.

No. 11. Elvira Cozzi, a pupil in the Benedictine convent of Teramo, was deprived of the power of speech, after a long and painful illness, and for five years and three months could not articulate a single word, nor even produce those guttural sounds generally possible to mutes. Her tongue had grown thick, numb and hardened, as though it were altogether dead. Recourse was had to the very best remedies: tonics, the water-cure, experiments with ether, chloroform and electricity: all to no avail. In despair, the doctors wished to try hypnotism, but this was not allowed them. Meanwhile the years passed by, and little Elvira seeing no chance of getting better, resigned herself to her hard lot, with rather bad grace. She invoked Our Lady under her various titles, made triduums and novenas to every patron saint, but without the least apparent advantage. Still, the nuns of the convent did not lose hope, for they dearly loved their young pupil. At last, some one spoke to them about the wonders wrought by the new servant of God, Gabriel, and they resolved to send her to his tomb, to be cured. She went to Isola with some of her relatives, and prayed long and frequently amid a great crowd of people. When her prayer was over, she prostrated herself on the marble tombstone and seemingly fell asleep. Her cousin approached her, put a few grains of the dust from Gabriel's grave into her mouth, and said to her: "Get up, Elvira, and cry out 'Saint Gabriel be praised!'" At that moment the girl awoke, and in a high, clear voice repeated over and over: "Saint Gabriel be praised!" The nerves and muscles of her tongue regained their former flexibility, and to this day she experiences no trouble in speaking, to the wonder and delight of all who knew her in the long years of her dumbness.

No. 12. Francis di Bernardo, of Bisenti, had accidentally contracted the horrible disease called cancerous syphilis. For thirteen months he lay on a bed of agony; exhausted, covered all over with sores like a leper, he was truly a loathsome and pitiable sight. Given up by the physicians, Bernard sought the help of the servant of God, and while invoking his intercession with confidence, he made use of a little of the dust from Gabriel's grave. Immediately he felt strength and vigor returning to his afflicted body, rose from his bed, and walked about without difficulty. He continued his novena of prayers, and on the eighth day, all his sores were closed and perfectly healed.

No. 13. Francis Marcantonio, of Morgia, aged twenty-two, was suffering from splenitis or inflammation of the spleen. His internal organs were likewise diseased, and he was enormously swollen by dropsy. Unable to find relief from doctors, he went to Gabriel's tomb, made an application of some of the miraculous dust, and was completely cured during the night of February 12, 1893, in the house of Bernard Castelli, where he was lodging.

No. 14. In the neighborhood of Ascoli Piceno, a certain woman was afflicted with a grievous cancer. She washed the diseased parts once with water, in which she had mixed some of the wonderful dust, and the cancer was healed. In the register kept at Isola, there is a long list of similar cures of every kind of cancer.

No. 15. In 1897, Violanta Moretti, of Rome, had been suffering from inflammation of the lungs of such a serious character, that she was given up by the doctors. She was actually in her last agony, and the attending priest was reciting the prayers for the dying. Josephine Alessandrini, a pious lady, then came into the room, and gave her dying friend some of the miraculous dust. No sooner did the patient take it, than she was instantly restored to perfect health.

No. 16. One evening in June, 1893, there came from Acquasanta to the retreat of Isola, a cripple named Anthony Mancini, who for many years had lost the use of his limbs in consequence of an obstinate arthritis. As the disease had crippled him in a frightful manner, the physicians attempted to straighten him, by breaking the joints of his thighs and knees; but this only completed his ruin, and deprived him of all hope of ever being able to take another step. Besides, the poor man was wasting away through muscular atrophy, so that he could no longer move his body, and was forced to spend his days seated in an armchair, from which he had to be lifted into bed at night.

Seated thus, and even bound in his chair, (lest the motion of the wagon should throw him off), he arrived after a long journey at the Passionist church. All who saw him were touched with deep compassion, and as he was moved from the wagon and carried to the tomb of the servant of God, many joined with him in prayer, asking his cure from God. During the night he was given lodgings in the abandoned retreat, and the next morning he was brought in his armchair into the church, to Gabriel's sepulchre. The parish priest of Isola having heard his confession and given him communion, the poor man continued his prayers to the servant of God. All at once, in the sight of all the people, Anthony rose from his chair cured, exclaiming: "Gabriel, the servant of God, has granted me the favor!" Leaving his chair behind him in the church, he got into his wagon unassisted, and joyfully turned his face homeward, blessing God. The people of the villages and towns through which he had passed on his way to Isola, and who had seen him in so pitiful a state, were now speechless with surprise on beholding him hale and hearty, and every now and then he had to stop and satisfy their wonder and curiosity.

No. 17. Not less extraordinary was the case of Cajetan Mariani, of Amatrice. In consequence of a stroke of apoplexy, he was paralyzed for twelve years in his whole body, so that he could barely drag himself around with the help of a cane. He was seventy-one years old, and entertained no hopes of being cured: still less did he think of praying, for he had lived estranged from his God for a long time. One day, by some unaccountable impulse, he desired to go to Isola. As he entered the monastery church, he saw a priest hearing confessions, and asked to be heard himself. The bystanders were greatly astonished at this, because they knew him well: greater still was their wonder, when they saw the old man making his confession with an abundance of tears. "A few days later," continues the priest, to whom we are indebted for these facts, "as I returned to the church, the man came up to me quite joyful, his eyes moistened with tears and said, 'Oh, Father, this dear servant of God obtained three great graces for me; he touched my heart and brought me back to my God. I have prayed, and felt myself cured all at once of my paralysis, so that I am well and can walk about with ease, you see; besides, I was afflicted for many years with a rupture: this too has disappeared this very hour! What shall I do to show my gratitude to God for so many blessings?'"

Whatever the enticing advertisements in our daily papers and circulating pamphlets, medical science tells us that the radical cure of rupture (hernia) is seldom accomplished except by operative surgery; and not a single instance has ever been recorded, of an instantaneous cure of hernia. Now we read in the processes, that Gabriel has declared himself by facts to be the *special* protector of the ruptured; and in 1897, we find on the register, about ninety cases of complete and instantaneous cure.

No. 18. It is not often that we find a person looking upon a severe physical discomfort as a blessing, or considering it a thing to be prayed for. The subjoined case is an exception to the general rule, and will explain itself.

A young Sicilian was drafted into the Italian army just before the late African campaign. Sicilians, as a rule, are not overanxious to leave their country, and let themselves be massacred for the glory of "unified Italy" into which they are incorporated to their disgust; but this young man felt particularly averse to running such a risk. He therefore besought Gabriel to come to his assistance, and on the very day when he was to present himself for the physical examination, there suddenly broke out a rupture of such gravity, that the poor conscript was declared permanently unfit for military service, and was discharged. But no sooner had he reached home, than every vestige of hernia disappeared, and he has since continued as sound and healthy as he had been before.

No. 19. The son of a druggist in Teramo had fallen sick so dangerously, that no remedy would avail, and he was at death's door. Already were the necessaries for the funeral being prepared, when the boy's parents bethought themselves of the recent miraculous recovery of a daughter of the military commander of the district, which wonderful cure had caused quite a sensation in the city. "Why," said they, "since that saint has so kindly shown favor to the girl's father, why shouldn't we trust that he will be equally kind to us?" So they prayed with great faith, and immediately their son was cured.

It may appear strange to some of our readers, that the boy's coffin was being made whilst he was still alive: but this practice is quite general in the remote mountainous province of the Abruzzi. No sooner does it become evident that one is in imminent danger of death, than a richly adorned casket is prepared; then, if by some supernatural intervention, the dying person is spared, the casket is carried to the sanctuary of the saint to whom they were indebted for the miraculous cure, and is left there as an *ex-voto* of gratitude and devotion. There are several of these caskets at Isola di Gran Sasso.

No. 20. It must indeed have been a touching spectacle, as an eyewitness relates, when one day there came down from the mountains, a little procession of persons, in the midst of whom was a figure all clothed in white. This was a twelve-year old boy, who with his father, mother, brothers and sisters, had come from a distance of thirty-six miles over a very rough road, all walking barefoot the whole way, and the dear little fellow carrying upon his head, the coffin in which he was about to be carried to the grave, had not Gabriel hastened to his assistance.

No. 21. Joseph Mary Albani, a young religious of the Order of the Servites of Mary, in the Convent of Saluzzo, was afflicted with pulmonary hemorrhages. The blood flowed from his mouth so frequently, and in such a quantity, that all remedies proved useless, and it was feared that he could not live long. By the advice of his physicians, who thought he might be benefited by a change of air, he was sent from Saluzzo to Rome, without however feeling any sensible improvement. In fact the young man was slowly wasting away, having lost all strength, appetite and sleep, and was quite unable to apply himself to any mental work. "When I visited him in Rome during the first days of April, 1893," writes F. Germanus, "I was moved with compassion. He seemed to be in the last stages of consumption, and was much reduced and exhausted. I advised him to recommend himself to Confrater Gabriel, and related to him several prodigies, which had lately occurred through his intercession. I gave him a picture of the servant of God, and a relic of his garments, which he applied with faith. Shortly afterward, he wrote to me from Naples, whither he had been sent, and said: 'I have made a novena in honor of your dear little saint. From the day I placed upon myself the image and relic, I have had no hemorrhages, and at present I feel perfectly cured. My appetite has returned, I have recovered my strength, and I am now able to apply to work better than before I got sick. I always carry about with me the picture of the servant of God, nor will I ever part with it.'

"In a subsequent letter, he says: 'It is now more than four months since I was cured, and I have not suffered from any return of my former disease. Your saint obtained that grace for me from the Blessed Virgin: I will show myself grateful to him, as long as I live.'"

No. 22. Sister Concetta of St. Michael, a religious of the convent of Capuchin Nuns at Santa Fiora in Tuscany, was wasting away from an ulcer in her stomach, which for five years had been extending, and was accompanied with all the painful phenomena usual in such cases. All human remedies had been resorted to unavailingly, and the attending physician himself despaired of giving relief. Yet, being a man of faith, after advising his patient to receive the last sacraments, he suggested that recourse be had to Confrater Gabriel, of whom he had heard so many wonders. A novena was made in consequence, by the whole community; and on its termination, a second one was commenced, all praying with the greatest confidence, except the poor patient herself, who instead of getting better, steadily became worse: in fact, at the end of the second novena, her misery seemed to have reached its climax. She was disheartened and prayed with coldness.

"Now," she relates herself, "just a little after midnight of the day, when the community commenced a third novena, (I know not whether I was awake or asleep) I heard someone calling me by name, in the sweetest voice I ever heard. Instantly the entire cell was filled with light, and in the midst of a bright globe I saw a most beautiful young man attired in black and wearing a surplice of dazzling whiteness. His face was far brighter and more radiant than the glory that encircled him. He drew near to my poor little bed, and I said: 'O good dear little Gabriel, won't you speak to me?' He answered: 'Are you not going to ask me for something?' 'Yes,' I said, 'give me what Mother Abbess wants me to have: cure me!' Then he touched me, and I was at once free from all pain. I thought I was in heaven both in soul and body, so great was the consolation I felt: I could not believe myself: 'Am I dreaming?' said I, as I sat up in bed, 'or what's the matter with me? I am cured!' And so indeed, it was. All this while, the servant of God was slowly withdrawing from the room, leaving me immersed in consolation."

"The dumb speak, the blind see, the deaf hear, the lepers are cleansed, the lame walk, and the devils are cast out." By these words, Christ our Lord announced His divine mission, and confounded the pride and hypocrisy of His enemies, by showing Himself to be the absolute Lord and Master of all nature. Luckily for our afflicted humanity, our merciful God still continues to work miracles through His Saints. Our warrant for believing this consoling doctrine is found in the Gospel of St. John 14:12, wherein Jesus Himself said: "Amen, amen, I say to you, he that believeth in Me, the works that I do, he also shall do; and greater than these shall he do." Therefore, the days of miracles can never be over.

We have seen instances of many different cures at Bl. Gabriel's tomb, and it is only our want of sufficient space that prevents our multiplying the record tenfold. There does not seem to be a single department of human misery, not a single disease or deformity, acute or chronic, even awful cases of diabolical possession, that God has not cured through the intercession and merits of the humble Passionist student, rightly surnamed the modern Thaumaturgus.

We have hitherto considered some miracles of God's *mercy* wrought in favor of Confrater Gabriel's clients; let us now bring this chapter to a close by narrating two miracles of God's *justice* avenging the honor of His servant attacked by impious men.

No. 23. In the province of Teramo there lived a man notorious for his bad life, and especially for his detestable habit of blaspheming. He was employed by a well-to-do family as driver, and it often devolved upon him to convey people to the tomb of the saintly young religious. Now, it happened one day, when he felt more than usually tired of these errands, that he flew into a passion, and began to utter all kinds of villainy against the servant of God, and all who believed in his miracles. But soon after this storm of profanity had passed away, he felt himself seized by an invisible hand, and thrown from his carriage to the ground, just as one would throw down something that he wished to dash to pieces. The man's horse ran off in a great fright, and it seemed as if both beast and vehicle would be utterly destroyed: but nothing of the kind happened: it was the driver alone who was injured. This poor man was picked up from the ground where he lay like one dead, all bruised and bleeding, particularly about his head. As God would have it, he regained consciousness and even recovered from the effects of his fall, but not completely. Day and night he continued to suffer in his head agonizing spasms of pain, that could not be mitigated: and he acknowledged himself, that had his torment lasted much longer, he would have taken his own life.

But God was willing to show him mercy, and cure him in soul as well as in body. Repenting of his fault, he repaired to the monastery church, and there with many tears besought God and His servant to pardon his blasphemies, promising to change his life. That very moment all his pain ceased, nor has it ever returned since. Andrew (for such is his name) has kept his promise, and mended his ways.

No. 24. A saloon-keeper of Campli obstinately persisted in ridiculing the many cures that happened in that neighborhood, in favor of such as had recommended themselves to Confrater Gabriel.

One day, urged on more than usual by the spirit of blasphemy, he went so far as to ridicule the servant of God himself with unbecoming jokes that scandalized all who heard him. Instantly, he lost his power of speech, being struck dumb; and what is worse, he has perversely remained in this unfortunate state ever since.

32 What Gabriel Has Done For Isola

"The poor church of the retreat at Isola will be one of the most illustrious sanctuaries of Italy,"—thus wrote F. Norbert on January 1, 1893, less than three months after the mortal remains of Gabriel Possenti had been brought to light; and surely the singular devotion that has since been seen about his tomb, and the number and character of the prodigies wrought there, bid fair to give the above assertion some semblance of prophecy.

When this saintly youth was still living upon earth, he seemed to be like a magnet, sweetly drawing to himself the hearts not only of his brethren in religion, but even of outsiders. All who came within the magic circle of his influence realized that "his conversation had no bitterness, nor his company any tediousness, but joy and gladness" (Wisdom 8:16): and this is now being daily renewed since the translation of his relics, and is perhaps the most remarkable of all the wonders wrought. Three years ago his name was almost forgotten; his body was interred in a common vault, in an abandoned monastery hidden away in the hills of the Abruzzi; now, it is echoed far and wide, it is on the lips and in the hearts not only of the common people, but of the princes of the church as well.

By reason of the persecution of the church in Italy, many of its inhabitants have remained for a long time without spiritual assistance and instruction, as can be seen from the many who come to our hospitable shores. The country around Isola had perhaps, more even than others, felt the sad consequences of spiritual neglect. "The churches were no longer frequented, the greater number of the people lived estranged from the sacraments, many had nothing left of their former Christianity but the mere name, or at most an external and wholly material religion. As to their morals, what shall I say? Blasphemy, drunkenness, licentiousness, and a host of vices that are ever the companions of infidelity, had increased beyond all proportion in every rank of society. I am not speaking of past centuries or even decades," writes F. Germanus, who supplies these details, "but of a state of things that existed a very short while ago, and to which thousands of persons can bear witness." This is the dark side of the picture: let us now glance at the other.

"Long processions are coming here from the villages all round about: their conduct gives great edification. Pilgrims are arriving every day. Despite the wintry season, they come from all distances to the tomb of Confrater Gabriel." Thus wrote a missionary scarcely two months from the date of the translation:[32] "All approach the sacraments," says Bishop Hippolytus, C.P., of Bulgaria (who had hastened to assist the missionary quoted above). "I can say from experience that even in a mission, the fruits of conversion and fervor daily seen here, could not be surpassed. I have sometimes questioned the people as to their motive in coming here, and received this answer: 'Since that saint has begun to manifest himself, a fear

---

[32] Editor's Note: The translation of St. Gabriel's remains to the new resting place.

and trembling has come over me on account of my sins, and please God, I'll sin no more.'" "The concourse of people is ever on the increase," writes another confessor: "penitents who for thirty or forty years had not practiced their duties, are now, with tears and regret for the past, desirous of being reconciled to God."

"Poor sinners!" a missionary writes, "they come on foot from distant villages, anxious to go to confession. They flock around me in the house, in the church, in the monastery, and in such numbers that were we five confessors instead of one, we could not hear them all. How sorry I feel to leave so many hundreds unabsolved! In the village here, and all its neighborhood," he continues, "faith has been revived, blasphemy and drunkenness have become unheard of, for these simple folk often say: 'In the presence of *san Gabriele*, and under his very eyes, it won't do to commit any more sins.' Truly, the servant of God has opened a mission for these neglected people, and there is reason to hope that it will last long."

O Isola! thou art not the least among the thousands, for Gabriel shall be thy glory! Buried but yesterday among thy hills, this holy servant of God is destined to be famous throughout the Christian world; and the children of the universal church will ere long come as pilgrims, from every Christian land to honor Gabriel Possenti, to display their faith and their gratitude in a sanctuary all his own, when the hour at last comes for his solemn canonization. May God hasten the day![33]

---

[33] Editor's Note: The Church solemnly canonized Saint Gabriel of Our Lady

33 His Solemn Beatification

Toward the end of the year 1894, the Superiors of the Congregation of the Passion deliberated about introducing the cause of the venerable servant of God for beatification and canonization, and in the following month, the compiling of the necessary documents began. The commission commenced its work in Spoleto, with the authorization of the Archbishop, for it was in that city that our Gabriel spent the first eighteen years of his life, until in fact he consecrated himself to the service of God in religion. From Spoleto the commission went to the dioceses of Terni, Rome, Albano, and lastly to Penne, where many lived who had known Gabriel well, and who were thus able to testify as to his virtues, and also as to the prodigies wrought by his intercession. Only thirty years had elapsed since his holy death; hence most interesting and important depositions could be expected from his three surviving brothers and sister, his former college companions, his masters, his brethren in religion, his confessor and spiritual director, who were alive when this first "episcopal process" was commenced. This first part of the work was duly finished in about a year, and the documents were laid before the Congregation of Rites, where all such causes are officially examined. The Cardinal Prefect of this Congregation himself took up the cause of Ven. Gabriel and became its chief advocate; so that it is wholly owing to his

---

of Sorrows on May 13, 1920.

loving energy that complete success was attained in a very short time.

At a meeting held on June 4, 1895, all the available writings of the servant of God were examined: his letters and a few of his compositions. Not only were they found free from theological errors or exaggerated piety, but it was unanimously voted that the solidity of their doctrine was as evident as their healthy common sense. Without delay the Holy See was then formally petitioned to allow the process of beatification and canonization to go forward: which if granted, would confer upon the servant of God the glorious title of "Venerable." Such a petition is usually made only by the most illustrious personages; and in our Gabriel's case it embraced all Europe, and nearly the whole Christian world, so eager did the foremost churchmen in every land appear to have the holy student's name enrolled upon the list of saints. Italy, France, Belgium, Spain, Portugal, Germany, Austria, England and Ireland, joined with the United States and Canada in an earnest entreaty to the Vicar of Christ, to allow the honors of the altar to be paid to the new servant of God. Ninety-nine such letters were received, thirty of which were written by Cardinals, thirty-five by Archbishops and Bishops, and thirty-four by Superiors General of Religious Orders. Every one of these documents addressed to the Holy See is a panegyric[34] in praise of an humble Passionist religious; every one of these illustrious writers becomes the voluntary champion of this young

---

[34] Editor's Note: A panegyric is a public speech or published text in praise of someone or something.

student, whose merits and virtues they all acknowledge, and whose power with God, they or their subjects have already experienced in private, and now ask to solicit in public. These ninety-nine letters would make a rare volume of most interesting reading; but our limits forbid their introduction here. Suffice it to say that on July 7, 1896, Pope Leo XIII graciously acceded to so many petitioners, and authorized the formal introduction of the Cause.

The next step was to examine whether the laws of the Church had been observed in the matter of worship; that is, whether *public* worship had been offered to the Ven. Gabriel; for it is forbidden to anticipate the judgment of the Church in such matters, and to treat any servant of God as if he had been already beatified or canonized. On January 5, 1897, it was officially declared that there was no hindrance on this score, and that the Cause could proceed in all safety. Hereupon the Pope showed most evidently his interest, and by apostolic decree, dispensed with the required proof of Gabriel's reputation for sanctity, saying: "It is as clear as the sun that his renown is at this moment spread abroad everywhere, and is increasing day by day." The "Apostolic Process" concerning Gabriel's virtues and miracles then commenced, one commission working in the diocese of Penne, a second in that of Teramo, and a third in Rome. Here again the Holy Father exhibited unusual interest in hastening the Cause of the holy young student. For the wisest of reasons, no Cause can be brought up for beatification sooner than fifty years after a person's death; besides which, ten years must elapse from the end of the first or episcopal

Process, to the introduction of the Cause before the Congregation of Rites. The Holy Father graciously dispensed with both laws, well knowing the extraordinary merits of the case. On July 23, 1902, the first of the three last meetings was held; the second on June 28, 1904; and the third and last on May 2, 1905 in the presence of the Pope. Eleven days afterward, he published a decree, solemnly declaring that there was no doubt but that Ven. Gabriel had exercised in a heroic degree the theological virtues of faith, hope and charity, as well as the cardinal virtues of prudence, justice, fortitude and temperance.

Then followed the examination of the miracles required by the laws of the Church as heaven's confirmation of the life and virtues of him who is to be canonized. Three were presented, viz: the instantaneous cure of the young woman Mary Mazzarella, of Isola di Gran Sasso, of consumption, described on page 220; the cure of Dominic Tiberi of Colliberti, of a most grievous rupture, described on page 225; and the perfect and sudden restoration to health of Sr. Mary of Our Lady of Pompeii, described on page 227.

Inasmuch as these three miracles were fully attested by eyewitnesses, for the most part, two miracles only were needed, according to the general practice of the Congregation of Rites, and the first two were selected. The examination was rigorous and prolonged, lasting over three years. All the witnesses and documents were patiently examined in private, and the results discussed in three public meetings convened for this special purpose. The Holy Father published the decree of approval of these miracles on January 26, 1908, and appointed the last day of May for the solemn enrolling of Gabriel's name among those declared Blessed.

Rejoice then, O Congregation of the Cross and Passion of our Bl. Redeemer, rejoice in the glory brought thee by this thy son! Many another hast thou brought forth and trained on Calvary, at the foot of the Cross where thou hast taken up thy dwelling. Many of these thy children have honored thee by the splendor of their heroic virtue, and by the merits of their long, laborious and most fruitful apostolate. But this angelic youth, Gabriel of the Sorrowful Virgin, has made thee in these latter days renowned among all the older Orders of the Church of God; for he has triumphantly shown how the observance of thy Rule enables the Christian soul to carry the cross of Jesus Christ to the highest reaches of perfection, and become the wonder and joy of the whole world.

As a fitting conclusion to this life of the Bl. Gabriel, the following description of the ceremony of beatification is appended.

The young Passionist student Francis Possenti was solemnly beatified in St. Peter's in Rome, Sunday, May 31, 1908. The greatest and grandest church in the world was made more magnificent still by the decorations used on the occasion. The light of day having been completely shut out, the vast interior was filled with the mellow radiance of twenty-five thousand electric lamps which were artistically arranged so as to recall the Passion of our Redeemer, and the seal of the Passionist Order. Hundreds of the glowing bulbs circled every arch, extended along every cornice, and were massed in gigantic candelabra. The walls were everywhere covered with costliest tapestry and gorgeous hangings of silk, relieved by large pictures of Bl. Gabriel, and the miraculous evidences of his power with God. Not only were the architectural lines and grand proportions of the building thus faithfully emphasized but St. Peter's actually looked like a new place: it was said to be bewilderingly beautiful.

Two files of soldiers cleared a passage up to the Altar of St. Peter's Chair (or the Confession, as it is styled) through a crowd that certainly numbered more than fifteen thousand persons of all nationalities. One faith, one hope and charity animated that vast assemblage, and lifted up their yearnings for one eternal home, even as it bowed their knees and minds to the profession of the same religion. In reverent wonder and expectation they clustered round the central altar of the basilica, to hear the decree which gave a young student of the Passionist Order the title of Blessed.

At 9:30 A.M., the procession started from the sacristy and on arriving at the altar, the Cardinals of the Congregation of Rites took their places on the gospel side. Card. Rampolla, the archpriest of St. Peter's basilica, who always presides at solemn functions celebrated there, was seated on the epistle side, surrounded by the Vatican Chapter and clergy, with many Archbishops and Bishops, and the higher superiors of the religious orders. When all were seated, the Postulator of the Cause of beatification, F. Germanus, C.P., accompanied by the Archbishop of Laodicea, Secretary of the Congregation of Rites, approached Card. Cretoni, Prefect of the same Congregation, and handed him the Apostolic Brief, asking him to order its publication. His Eminence consented, and sent them to ask the permission of Card. Rampolla to publish it in his church. Next, the Brief was read aloud, wherein the Holy Father, after praising the virtues of Ven. Gabriel declared him enrolled among the Blessed in heaven.

Then all present, Cardinals, bishops, priests and faithful rose to their feet; the painting of the newly beatified (which until then had been draped) was uncovered, the electric lights were turned on in greater profusion, the bells of St. Peter's pealed joyously, and the Te Deum, the church's hymn of praise and thanksgiving, was rapturously sung by the multitude present. The portrait and relic were next incensed, and solemn pontifical mass celebrated. A special platform was erected near the altar on which was seated Dominic Tiberi, who had been miraculously cured through the servant of God's intercession; and Gabriel's own brother, Dr. Possenti of Camerino, was also there, with several of his relatives. Round about the altar were many who had known the young saint intimately—some of his old fellow students, the aged F. Norbert who was Gabriel's spiritual director,—and even the lady, now the wife of an officer in the Italian army, who had once thought it such a great pity that Gabriel, then plain Francis, turned his back on the world and herself, to become a Passionist religious.

Blessed Gabriel in Glory

In the afternoon of the same day, another grand ceremony took place, when the Holy Father, Pope Pius X, came down from his private apartments to venerate the newly beatified. The function was announced for three o'clock, but long before that hour the piazza of St. Peter's was thronged with people. At two P.M., the great doors were thrown open, and a multitude of more than thirty thousand took their places in the largest church in the world.

At three o'clock the procession moved from the chapel of the Bl. Sacrament. A cross came first, attended by a large number of boys in white soutanes. Then followed the members of the different religious orders in their picturesque and graceful habits. It took some time for this part of the procession to pass. The variety of colors and costume, the changing expression of countenance in such a venerable army of men who had sacrificed the world and its glory to live in heroic self-denial was a striking scene, especially to those who came from lands where the habit of the religious is hardly ever seen outside their respective monasteries.

Then came the cross of the secular clergy, followed by all the parish priests of Rome, as well as the Canons of the various Basilicas. Next, the Roman Court in all its magnificence appeared with the members of the diplomatic corps accredited to the Holy See, together with the Roman nobility. A subdeacon came next bearing the papal cross, followed by many Archbishops and Bishops from all parts of the world. After them walked twenty-two Cardinals, and finally the elevated chair (or sedia gestatoria) on which the Pope was borne, surrounded by the noble guard as immediate attendants on the Supreme Pontiff. As soon as the venerable figure of Pius X was in full view, there was a wave in that sea of humanity, now falling and then rising as the crowd knelt to receive the papal blessing.

Only in the Catholic church can one witness such a sight. In that mighty throng of thirty thousand, there were men of every profession, from all ranks in society, standing reverently side by side with ordinary men and women from nearly every nation under the sky. On looking at them gathered round the Vicar of Christ, one naturally thought of that multitude that no man can number, of all peoples and tribes and tongues, together with the choirs of glorified spirits who assist about the throne of the Most High.

When this grand and absolutely matchless procession came to the altar, the relic of Bl. Gabriel was exposed; hundreds of candles were lighted, and tens of hundreds of electric lights turned on. Lastly, when the Bl. Sacrament was likewise exposed, the choir sang the hymn in honor of the newly beatified. This being ended, the invocation rang out in clear and thrilling tones *for the first time in public*: "Pray for us, O Blessed Gabriel!" and like the sound of many waters came the universal response: "That we may be made worthy of the promises of Christ." The prayer from the newly approved office followed and closed the official ceremony.

The feast of Bl. Gabriel has been fixed for May 31, the last day of Mary's month,—as though the Church wished her children to have a perpetual reminder of one of the greatest causes of Gabriel's sanctity,—his tender, lifelong devotion to the Blessed Mother of God.[35] Surely in this we can all imitate him. When we reflect on the dangers through which our hero passed, and then consider the greatness and grandeur of his triumph even here upon earth, we ought to be inspired to seek safety from the snares and temptations of the same world, where he did,—that is, under the mantle of Our Lady of Sorrows, who is also the Mother of Grace.

---

[35] Editor's Note: The Church has since moved St. Gabriel's feast day to February 27th, the date of his holy death.

Made in the USA
Middletown, DE
28 October 2024

63488982R00144